WHO AM I NOW?

Growing Through Life's Changing Seasons

WHO AM I NOW?

Growing Through Life's Changing Seasons

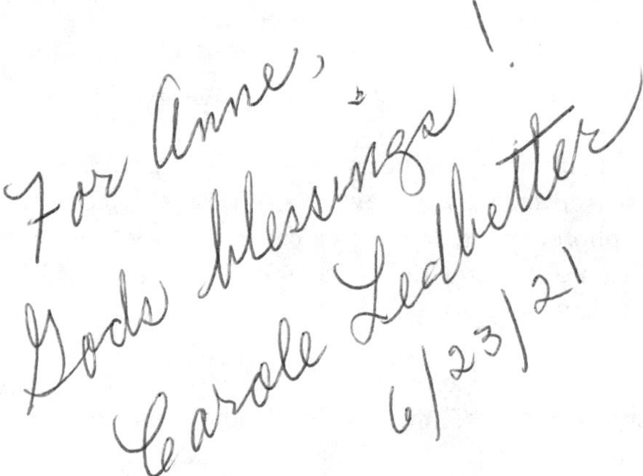

Carole Ledbetter

Published by Redemption Press, PO Box 427, Enumclaw, WA 98022.

The material in this book is appropriate for either personal or group study. Questions in the "Things to Think About and Discuss" sections will be particularly helpful for group study.

ISBN 13: 978-1-63232-709-3

Library of Congress Catalog Card Number: 2006908987

Table of Contents

Preface: Women Sharing the Adventure

Summer 1998

For nearly ten years I had been teaching teenagers in my local church. Our own teenagers had grown up, completed their education, married, and established homes of their own. We had four wonderful grandchildren! (We now have six.)

I enjoyed teaching teens. I loved their enthusiasm and zest for life. I watched them grow and change.

After our church hired a youth pastor, I thought it must be time for me to leave the youth group. I asked God what I should do next. I read the second chapter of the Book of Titus, where the Bible says older women should teach younger ones. Was I now an "older" woman? Would any younger woman want to listen to me?

I looked in the mirror; sure enough, an "older" woman looked back at me. (She smiled, wondering that I hadn't noticed her before.) Amazing, isn't it, how the term "older" takes the sting out of "old." Where had the time gone? About that time, my pastor approached me and asked, "Have you ever thought of teaching a women's class?"

I was ready for a new adventure.

We called ourselves "Ladies of Grace."

Eighteen-year-old, Lisa, a college student, often sat next to Nellie, age ninety-three, as we shared truth, prayer requests, sorrows, encouragement, laughter, and stories from our separate journeys.

Together we viewed life's various stages, listened, and considered differing points of view while we learned from the past and the present. We discovered biblical patterns and principles that are timeless and relevant, and we found joy in our mutual search.

This book is a result of the discussions we held and the truths we discovered.

Introduction: Who Do You Think You Are Anyway?

Who am I now? I frequently ask myself.

I seem always to be changing.

I have been a child, a daughter, a sister, a teenager, a bride, a wife, a mother, a seeker of truth, a believer in Christ, a Bible teacher, a secretary, a bank officer, a musician (of sorts), a grandmother, a Welcome Wagon representative, a home-decorating consultant, a writer, a newspaper columnist, a public speaker, and a friend.

Women live their lives sequentially—we are first one thing and then another, with many overlapping roles.

I've played many of these roles simultaneously. So have you.

Have you ever asked yourself who you really are?

What are your thoughts, your dreams, your worries, your disappointments?

How do you see yourself?

And a bigger question: how does God see you?

Right now—where you are.

And tomorrow?

Who will you be then?

Just who do you think you are anyway?

Identity: It's who we think we are. It's how we see ourselves and how we see God.

As children, we get our self-image from our parents, teachers, coaches, relatives, and friends—those who comment about us, laugh at us, approve of us, or disapprove of us, judge us, favorably or not, those who love us, and those who withhold their love.

Later on we make our own judgments. We dream what we'll be, what we'll do. And then the disappointments come. Life doesn't turn out the way we thought it would. We fail because failing is part of life too.

We seem always to be waiting for someone to tell us who we are.

And then there is God. Where is He? Can we find Him? Or will He find us? Are we already searching for Him in our own quirky kind of way? Is He searching for us?

Only the God who created us knows who we were meant to be. Our lives reflect how we see God, and our relationship to Him defines everything else in our lives.

CHAPTER ONE

I'M A BELIEVER

The Race

As the early morning sun beat down on what promised to be another hot June day, Marcy waited to sign up for the race. Anticipating the adrenaline rush she'd felt in a number of other local community-sponsored races, she couldn't wait to begin. She had run the staked-out course, clocked her speed, and limbered her muscles for many mornings in preparation for this event. Now her heart pounded with readiness as she looked forward to the sound of the starting gun.

Since it was a charity race, the registration fees would help handicapped children. The fifteen-dollar entry fee also covered a t-shirt, which she would add to her growing collection.

As she reached the registration table, a pleasant woman greeted her, handing her the required entry form. "Are you entering the race, or did you just want the t-shirt?" she asked. Surprised, Marcy asked her to explain. She learned that the committee had decided to give a t-shirt to anyone contributing fifteen dollars, even if they had no intention of running the race.

Her comment led Marcy think about her Christian faith: "Am I in the race, or did I only sign up for the t-shirt?" she asked herself.

Observing the manner in which the Christian gospel is often presented, one would assume that the beginning of our faith is the end. We encourage seekers to confess that they are sinners and receive Christ into their lives by praying a simple prayer. We encourage them to read their Bibles, pray, go to church as often as possible, tell others about their new faith, and adopt the lifestyle of the Christians around them (hoping they will copy the ones who meet with our approval).

But many remain at the starting gate. They have heard that Jesus "paid it all," but they believe they are now expected to "shape up" by their own effort. When they try and fail day after day, they become convinced that God is disappointed with them, and their guilt goes unresolved. It's uncomfortable to be around God. They can't meet His standards. So they drift away, thinking that, for them at least, it just doesn't work.

They don't realize that Christ's righteousness has been credited to them and they now stand before God forgiven and clean and that the Holy Spirit wants to begin producing His fruit in their lives.

When we enter the family of God through an initial step of belief, our salvation is complete, but it is not "all over." We begin a race, a relationship, and a journey that lasts a lifetime and beyond. (See Hebrews 12:1–2.)

We must discard whatever hinders us (habits, relationships, wrong ideas, etc.).

We must persevere (don't grow weary) in the race *marked out for us*.

We must look in faith to Jesus, who will perfect our faith (bring us to maturity).

Our salvation began in eternity past, says Romans 8:29–30, and God will continue that work until we are glorified in His presence.

It's *more than* a prayer; it's a life.

He is *more than* the author of our faith; He is the finisher.

He has done *more than* take away our sins; He justified us and gave us His righteousness.

It's *more than* Heaven when we die; it's abundant life now.

It's *more than* John 3:16; it's claiming all the promises of God's Word.

It's *more than* another witnessing formula; it's creating a craving for Christ in others.

The Relationship

If you are married, think back to your wedding day. Picture yourself and your new husband driving away from the church, tin cans clinking from the rear bumper and Just Married signs plastered on your car. You are entering a joyous new phase in your life. As a result of the vows you have taken, you are assuming new loyalties, privileges, and responsibilities.

Becoming a believer in Christ similarly creates new relationships, with accompanying loyalties, privileges, and responsibilities. Becoming a Christian can, in some ways, be compared to getting married. Things do not remain the same.

The apostle Paul, in the seventh chapter of Romans, declares that the Christian died to the law and now belongs to Christ (Romans 7:4–6).

Believers become a part of Christ's bride, the church.

In Romans 3:21–26, we learn righteousness has been provided for us by God and that it is acquired through faith in Jesus Christ. We don't achieve this righteousness by our own effort. We have sinned, but we are made right with God through Christ's sacrifice of Himself on the cross. God's justice has been satisfied, and those who believe in Jesus are now acceptable to God. The goal was not only to take away our sin—He had to do that first—but that we could experience new life in Christ.

We begin by believing in Jesus, placing our faith in Him, trusting Him; and that faith is a gift of God (Ephesians 2:8–10). (See also John 6:28–29, 35–37, and 44.) Only God can cause someone to be born again by His Spirit. We cannot make it happen by persuasion or saying "magic" words.

Believers are baptized into Christ's death (Romans 6:1–7). In other words, when Jesus died, we died *with* Him, even though we were not yet born. What a mysterious and wonderful truth! Our old life is gone. When we believe in Christ, we exchange our lives for His, and we begin anew! As we begin to *see* (consider) ourselves in this way, both our thinking and our behavior change.

We become new people, born again into a relationship with Christ and His church. Our initial surrender is followed by an unfolding of our new lives in Him. One big yes is followed by many small ones. It is long obedience in the same direction.

The Journey

When Jesus called His disciples to follow Him, it involved a major life change. Fishermen left their nets and tax collectors changed their occupations. Their lives were never the same after they responded to Jesus' call.

The verb, "follow," indicates one is going somewhere. Old habits and ways of thinking are left behind. New adventures lie ahead.

We are called to be changed by the changeless God.

We are called to be His followers.

Followers are learners, another word for *disciple.*

We are called to become like Jesus Christ.

Our journey can begin with a simple prayer of faith, but a journey is composed of many steps, not just one. Romans 1:17 declares, "For in the gospel a righteousness from God is revealed, a righteousness that is by faith from first to last, just as it is written: 'The righteous will live by faith.'"

Living by faith requires *seeing* ourselves as new people, daily *yielding* to the one we are following, and *obeying* biblical principles.

The spirituals captured the idea in their titles, "My Lord, I'm On My Journey" and "Get on Board, Li'l Children." There is a journey, and *the beginning is for the purpose of getting started.* A free ticket doesn't necessarily mean we have boarded the train.

Jesus calls us to come, believe, learn, trust, follow, and adventure in His will.

Jesus is described as "the author and *perfecter* of our faith" (Hebrews 12:2). In Philippians 1:6, we are promised He will carry it on to completion.

People sometimes speak of "making a decision," referring to a time when they prayed a prayer of commitment to Christ. But there may be little or no evidence of being in the race, in relationship to Christ or His church, or being on the journey. Perhaps they do not understand what it is they have decided. Faith is ongoing and active, leading to life in the truth. Saving faith will change the way we think and live. It is *a birth to a life* of growth and freedom—a grand adventure, perhaps more a discovery than a decision. The word *belief* comes from "by-lief" or "by-life." Your beliefs are the things you believe in sufficiently to act upon, to live by.[1] There is no entry fee. The fare has been paid. God provides everything you need along the way. But if you remain at the starting gate, you will miss the *race*, the *relationship*, the *journey*, and the desired destination.

Suppose I invite you to my party and you say, "Yes, I'd love to come. I accept the invitation." But you do not come. You never taste the culinary delights I have prepared for you. You never share in fellowship with other guests. You never experience the joy of the party.

Did you really accept my invitation?

Scripture Passages to Consider

- Matthew 13:1–30
- Ephesians 1:1–14; 2:4–10
- Romans 3, 6–8
- 1 Corinthians 9:24–27
- John 3:1–21; 6:26–50
- Hebrews 12:1–2
- James 1:18
- 2 Corinthians 5:17

Things to Think About or Discuss

- Describe how your relationship with Christ began.
- What first drew you to Him? Why did you come?
- What happened next?
- How did your thinking change?
- What life changes took place?
- How important is obedience in a continuing walk of faith?
- What part do the Scriptures play in your continuing growth?
- What promises did you learn to depend on?
- As you look back, what are some of the highlights of your journey?
  1. Where were the hard places?
  2. Where did you grow the most?
  3. What do you think a person coming to Christ in an initial act of faith needs to know?

SEEING OURSELVES IN CHRIST

Those who believe in Christ no longer stand before God as guilty sinners. We died *with* Christ and were *raised with Him* to new life. Jesus is now seated at the right hand of God and believers are united with Him. This may be beyond our understanding, but it is not beyond our believing, because it is true.

The Bible says God sees believers as being "in Christ." To be in Christ is to be accepted by God, not on our own merit but on the merit of Christ. Our sin has been credited to Christ and His righteousness credited to us—even though we did nothing to deserve it. It is the most wonderful fact in the new believer's life. God now sees us justified by Christ's death, possessing His righteousness, and indwelt by His Holy Spirit.

The more we learn to see ourselves as God sees us, the more joyous and fulfilling our lives will be.

While we still have sinful desires, we can now choose to follow Jesus in our daily pursuits and live above the temptations that bring us frustration and sin.

The "rats" of our sinful nature will continue to live in the basements of our beings, tempting us to stray from Christ, but we can learn to live on the first floor, yielding to God, rising above the sins that would defeat us. God works in us both to *will and to do* what pleases Him. As we continue to trust God's wisdom and sovereignty, we will desire to live in a manner that pleases Him. Why wouldn't we?

To Those Who Are not Yet in Christ

If you have never placed your personal faith in Jesus, trusting His death as payment for your sin, you are not "in Christ." You are lost and not in a right relationship to God, because your sins stand in the way. Jesus said that all who come to God must come through Him, a shocking truth to people who feel they can choose the manner in which they approach a holy God.

If God has put within you a desire to believe and follow Jesus, you can open your mind, heart, and life to Him at this moment. You can welcome Him into your life in simple childlike faith. Yes, it's scary to allow someone else to be in control of your life, but this is what God wants from us, to believe and follow—keep learning, keep following—for a lifetime! His Holy Spirit will illumine your mind and enable you to believe and give you understanding as you study the Bible.

Jesus, the Creator God, made you, loves you, and wants to live His life in you. When you launch on life's greatest adventure, that of knowing God, you will begin to become the *real you*, the person God intended you to be.

Will you invite Him into your life today, before continuing in this book? Simply—in your own words—ask Christ to forgive your sin, come into your life, and make you a new person—right now.

If you have invited Christ into your life, you will want to begin studying the Bible. As the Holy Spirit speaks to you through the Bible, you will begin to understand your new identity as a believer in

Jesus Christ. Finding a church where the Word of God is believed and taught will also help you grow spiritually.

The verses following will help you see yourself in Christ.

How God Sees Believers

- John 15:14–16: We are Jesus' friends. He chose us; we didn't choose Him. He appointed us to bear fruit.
- Galatians 3:7–9: We are children of Abraham, Abraham's "seed."
- Galatians 3:25–29: We are sons of God through faith in Christ Jesus, no longer under supervision of the law.
- Galatians 4:7–9: We are not slaves but sons and heirs. We are known by God.
- Galatians 5:4: We are free from trying to be justified by law.
- Galatians 5:22–23: We are free to produce the fruit of the Holy Spirit: love, joy, peace, patience, kindness, goodness, faithfulness, gentleness, self-control.
- Ephesians 1:3–14: We were chosen in Him to be holy and blameless, predestined to be adopted in accordance with *His* pleasure and according to His plan. We were included in Christ. We were marked with the seal of the Holy Spirit, guaranteed an inheritance, to be redeemed as God's possession.
- Ephesians 2:1: We were (past tense) dead in transgressions and sins, but are now made alive in Christ (verse 5).

- Ephesians 2:6: We were raised up with Christ, seated with Him in heavenly realms.
- Ephesians 2:10: We are His workmanship (not workmen), created to do good works, which God prepared in advance for us to do.
- Ephesians 2:19: We are fellow citizens with God's people, members of God's household.
- Ephesians 2:22: We are built together to become a dwelling in which God lives.
- Colossians 1:22: We are reconciled by Christ's body, holy in his sight.
- Colossians 2:12: We have been buried with Him in baptism and raised with Him.
- Colossians 3:2–4: We died and our life is now hidden with Christ in God. When Christ appears, we will appear with Him in glory.

CHAPTER TWO

I'M A WOMAN

Did you know that your birth was not your beginning? You didn't even begin at conception. You began before the creation of the world as an idea in the mind of God. Your body, yet uncreated, was planned by God. He chose the time you would be born; He chose your parents, your hair color, your talents and abilities. If you're not sure about this, read Psalm 139:13–16 and Ephesians 1:3–14.

Let's look at who God is and how He created mankind, both men and women.

"In the beginning, God…," says Genesis 1:1.

It all begins with God, the Creator, the Sustainer, the Holy One.

Did you know that because of the Hubble telescope and its tremendous power, scientists are discovering new galaxies? I believe that because God is a creator, He is constantly creating—it's what He does. He is the all-powerful one, the sovereign God, the creator God, and the one who loves us!

Many years ago, while on my knees scrubbing the dining room floor, I first heard George Beverly Shea sing, "Tenderly He Watches,"[1] a song that says we were part of God's plan long before the beginning of time. I was fifteen years old and my mother had died a few months earlier. When I heard that song coming over the radio, I realized God was watching over me and He had a wonderful, although sometimes difficult, plan for my life. He had known me before time began, and would continue to watch over me. I felt as if God were talking just to me that day.

Notice the following in the Genesis 1 portion:

1. *Mankind* is plural (just as God is plural "let *us* make man in *our* image"). (By the way, God wasn't lonely, nor did He *need* mankind. Within the Trinity—Father, Son, and Holy Spirit—there was perfect unity and joy.) But woman wasn't an afterthought; she was part of God's original plan. Both men and women constituted "mankind," and they were to rule together over the world of nature God created.
2. She was created as man's equal, also in God's image. Men and women were created to complement each other. (Not "compliment," as in say nice things, although that's not a bad idea either.) To complete one another—to become one.
3. Woman wasn't created for a *specific* man. (Except in Eve's case.) It is not true that every woman was created to be married. Single women are not "unclaimed blessings" but are created to glorify God, just as women who are called to be married are created to glorify God. The Bible indicates some people can glorify God better in a single life. (See 1 Corinthians 7:8.)

Women have varying gifts, just as men do. Some women in Bible times held positions of leadership: Esther was a queen, Deborah, a judge. Jael was a warrior who drove a stake through the head of a soldier! (I hope I never have to do that, don't you?) Priscilla and Aquila, her husband, ministered side by side to instruct new believers. Lydia was a church planter in her city. In modern times women such as Indira Ghandi of India and Margaret Thatcher in Great Britain have been competent leaders. Condoleeza Rice and Hillary Clinton have been suggested as possible presidential candidates in the United States.

Jesus paid high tribute to women by honoring His mother and maintaining friendships with the women who believed in Him, honored Him, followed Him, and ministered to Him, even coming to the tomb after His resurrection. It was to a woman that Jesus first revealed Himself following His resurrection. Countries where the Christian gospel has gone place women in higher esteem than countries where other religions predominate.

In Genesis 2, we read that marriage makes the man and woman one flesh in God's eyes, and they are instructed to leave their first families (parents) and cleave to each other.

We'll explore more about marriage in later chapters.

What Does It Mean to Be a Christian Woman In Today's World?

Our culture is rapidly changing. Most women today work at jobs outside their homes. Many will not have the privilege of staying at home with their children as their mothers and grandmothers did in years past. Many wouldn't choose to do that, even if conditions in their lives made it possible. The pace of life has quickened as women have attempted to be successful in the workplace, at home, and in the community.

Television, movies, magazines, peers, people in the workplace, sports figures, and celebrities of various sorts all influence women today. Many women live far away from their families and the places they grew up. According to recent polls, the church exerts little influence in terms of actual lifestyle choices.

But, according to the Bible, women still retain their primary biblical roles as teachers, keepers of their homes, and lovers of their husbands, children, and others whom God places in their lives. Women preserve the stories, the family histories and traditions. Women grieve over broken relationships and attempt to repair them. Women pray over those who have not yet come to faith in Christ and those who have strayed from Him. This is not to say that men don't value these things too, but relationships are our specialty!

Who Influences Women Today

Women are influenced by magazines, TV, movies, newspapers, talk shows, soap operas, their families, and—probably most of all—by their peers.

Our world tells us:

- Beauty is the ultimate goal.
- You must have the latest styles in clothing, cars, and home furnishings.
- You and your needs come first. Women should seek self-fulfillment.
- Live now. It's the only time you have.
- Caring for children is tedious and boring. Every woman needs a career.

- An educated woman should not have to cook, clean, or care for a husband.
- Women need to assert their rights in order to demonstrate their equality to men.
- Chastity before marriage and faithfulness in marriage are out-of-date ideas.
- No one should tell anyone else what to do.
- You have the right to decide what is right or wrong. There are no absolutes.

These values and viewpoints of the world bombard us constantly. I want to encourage women in the twenty-first century to assist one another in finding biblical principles for their various roles and relationships. I want to inspire older women and younger women to share their ideas and to listen and learn from one another.

Titus 2:3–5 says "Teach the older women to be reverent in the way they live, not to be slanderers, or addicted to much wine, but to teach what is good. Then they can train the younger women to love their husbands and children, to be self-controlled and pure, to be busy at home, to be kind, and to be subject to their husbands, so that no one will malign the Word of God."

In the King James Version of the Bible, the phrase, "to be busy at home," translates as keepers at home or keepers *of* the home. (It doesn't mean you can't go anywhere!) In this passage, women are assigned three roles: *teachers* (older teaching younger), *keepers* of their homes, and *lovers* of their husbands and children.

Although today a large percentage of women are employed outside their homes, these roles remain primary.

Paul, the writer of the Book of Titus, calls himself an apostle of Jesus Christ "for the faith of God's elect and the knowledge of the truth that leads to godliness...." (Titus 1:1).

Faith in God's truth leads to godliness. The principles set forth in Paul's time, when applied today, will lead to godly lives.

Why should we desire to live godly lives? Because God loves us and His Word holds the answers to our deepest needs and desires.

At the time the apostle Paul wrote, there were many who were insubordinate, empty talkers, and deceivers who caused people to turn away from the truth (Titus 1:10).

He stresses the importance of teaching sound doctrine (Titus 2:1). If doctrine is unimportant, truth is unimportant. Right thinking precedes right living. Who would give his life for that which is not true? We must love God with our minds, as well as our hearts and souls.

Older Women Teach By Example

We teach by example, first of all. Our lives should demonstrate that "being" is more important than "doing." Qualities such as holiness, respect, and reverence must characterize our lives if we are to influence others.

When we grow older and our families no longer require the bulk of our time, we may be tempted to despair; to idleness; to "hiding," in addictions like shopping, eating, sleeping, or substance abuse; or we may develop a critical spirit, becoming "busybodies" in the lives of others.

As the world around us changes, we may think things were better as they used to be. We can become critical and resist new ideas. Although not all change is good, growth can't take place without it. Because God holds the master plan for our lives, we can trust Him and embrace the changes that come to us.

Older women must not become slanderers, says the Bible. Why is this sin mentioned? Is it because we are apt to criticize those who do things differently from the way we do them?

Philippians 4:8 encourages us to think about what is positive and praiseworthy and to shun gossip and fault-finding. Critical attitudes prevent younger women from listening to our counsel and profiting from our example. We have much to gain by listening and learning from one another.

In a world that mocks the good, we can demonstrate it through lives that are godly, self-controlled, and amiable.

Teaching How to Love

Perhaps now, as in no other time, we need to learn how to love. Discovering ways to love our husbands that include homemaking, encouragement, companionship, and sexual intimacy can be a fulfilling adventure.

Loving our children challenges us to provide security, instruction in godliness, and an environment conducive to their spiritual, physical, mental, and moral development.

Daily we read about child abuse and neglect. Divorce and single-parent homes are common in our society. Teenagers roam our streets with nowhere to go. The idea of serving others is looked down upon by many. Yet the Bible encourages us to find fulfillment in serving our families and others. Older women can help by teaching, encouraging, and assisting younger women and single parents as they care for their children. Jesus never considered serving to be demeaning.

We can allow our culture to control our thinking, or we can allow Christ to transform us through the renewing of our minds (Romans 12:1–2).

The Holy Spirit's rule in our lives will result in purity, kindness, self-control, and beauty that doesn't come from fashions, the fitness center, or copying celebrities, but from the inner self, a gentle and quiet spirit, which is of great worth in God's sight (1 Peter 3:3–4). Attractive hairdos and fashionable clothing are not wrong, but God places greater value on the beauty of *a quiet, gentle spirit.*

Keepers of the Home

Being keepers of our homes prevents our days from being idle and empty. Magazine articles relating to homes and families still interest women with careers more than any other topic "even though many women today are working and pursuing their careers, and are very educated, deep within their souls is another voice. It is the relational voice that springs forth when they want reading material. Even though they may have other interests and vocations, their ultimate fantasy is that of the home and the relationships cultivated there," according to Cynthia and Robert Hicks, authors of *The Feminine Journey, Understanding the Biblical Stages of a Woman's Life.*[2]

A woman sets the emotional tone of her home. The quote, "If Mama ain't happy, ain't nobody happy," is true. Women hold valuable keys to the emotional well-being of their families

Learning to Love

We must learn to be lovers—lovers of God, our husbands, our children, and the people of our world. It's a big assignment and an important one.

Jesus commanded in Matthew 22:37–39: "Love the Lord your God with all your heart and with all your soul and with all your mind...Love your neighbor as yourself." Yes, we are also to love ourselves. When we possess the kind of self-love that Jesus had in mind, we will be able to love others with His kind of love. God's kind of love is unconditional, accepting, pure, and self-sacrificing. It is not the shallow, sentimental, self-gratifying kind of love portrayed by today's media. God's love changes people.

When our homes and families model God's thinking, we will find contentment and be able to influence the world around us in a positive way.

Things to Think About or Discuss

- What does it mean to be feminine?
- What are some qualities that define women?
- What makes you glad you are a woman?
- What limitations do you feel because you are a woman?
- What woman in your life has influenced you the most?
- Review the statements in this chapter that begin "Our world tells us…"
- How would you respond to each of them?

CHAPTER THREE

I'M A WIFE

Eve Had the First One—a Husband, That Is

The woman rubbed her eyes to shield them from the all-encompassing brightness. Freshly formed by the hand of the Creator God, she was new and infused with His life. The warmth of Divine Presence and approval enveloped her. Clothed with the joy of being, she looked about as she beheld the breathtaking beauty of the garden.

And then she saw the man, not far off. "Who is that?" she asked.

"That is Adam. I made you for each other. You are to be his helper, his wife."

"What's a wife?"

"Someone to complete him, to meet his needs, be his other half. Together you will be mankind—male and female. He will be called a husband."

"What will we do in this new place?"

"It's called Earth. Together you will begin to populate it. You will become the mother of all living."

"You mean there will be other people?"

"Yes, there will be babies. The two of you will live in My presence and fulfill My purpose on the earth."

"What a great idea!"

"You will be called woman. But you will also have a name. Adam will decide that. Confidentially, he's thinking of calling you Eve."

"Hmm, Eve...I like that. Short, but feminine."

"You were taken from him, you know. You are a part of him—taken from his side, made from his rib."

"He looks splendid for having so recently undergone surgery. When can I meet him?"

"Let Me bring you to him now. He will love you and care for you, and together you will care for the earth that I have made."

Theirs was a marriage made in Heaven. They were made for each other, literally. The first husband, Adam, the prototype for all to follow; Eve, his wife—a gift to him—a helper, perfectly suited to him by the Creator God.

In Genesis, chapters one and two, we read that God blessed them and commanded them to be fruitful. They were to "leave and cleave." (Although there were no parents or prior family to leave behind.) Perfectly suited to one another, they were "*one*"—mankind: male and female. Naked and unashamed, their intimacy was celebratory and wholesome.

But because of their willful disobedience, sin entered the world. Division and blame resulted. God judged them.

(See Genesis chapter 3.) Adam's work became drudgery. Now clothed in animal skins, their complete openness was gone. In shame, they were expelled from the perfect environment of the garden. Painfully Eve brought forth sons, who later competed for God's favor. Brotherly hostility resulted in violence and murder. Utopia was gone.

In the years that followed, with the garden a beautiful memory and daily toil a tedious reality, grieving for her sons in the anguish of bringing forth other children, perhaps Eve wondered: "How will we find our way back to God? How will we care for this place called Earth? How can Adam and I become one, when there is so little understanding between *us* now? How will I care for this person called a husband?"

How Do You Care for a Husband?

Eve may have been the first to consider this question, but she was not the last. Women since then have answered it in differing ways.

A generation or two ago, when most people lived on farms, our grandmothers prepared huge meals for their husbands and other farm workers. Caring for a husband then included many tasks wives do not do today, such as daily baking bread, washing clothes with the aid of a washboard or a wringer washer, and tackling heaps of ironing.

Many women today frown on "taking care" of anyone. They work at jobs outside their homes and expect household responsibilities, such as cooking and cleaning, to be divided equally. No matter how these tasks are divided, certain biblical principles do not change.

Biblical teaching concerning the care of a husband seems to center around two basic needs: *love* and *respect*.

Let's look at love first of all. According to 1 Corinthians 7:3–5, one of the ways marital love is shown is through sexual relationship. The passage indicates that partners are not to deprive one another of marital privileges but that sex is an important part of marriage. When we deny our husbands in this area, except by mutual agreement (mentioned in verse 5), we are disobedient to God. A husband loves to know that he is desired by his wife.

"Sexual yearnings aren't part of the fall," says M. Craig Barnes, "God created us that way. What our bodies yearn for is symptomatic of the yearning of our soul."[1] Barnes believes the church should talk more about sexuality because the Bible does. "When we have sex, we're not just touching a body; we're touching a soul," he says.

Because sex is holy, the Bible teaches it should be confined to marriage.

But husbands (and wives) need to be loved in other ways too—through affection, admiration, thoughtful deeds, cooperation, and understanding. (And never underestimate home-cooking. Remember, the adage that the way to a man's heart is through his stomach!)

Gary Chapman, in his book, *The Five Love Languages*, says, "We must be willing to learn our spouse's primary love language if we are to be effective communicators of love."[2]

In his book, Chapman lists the five "love languages" as:

1. Words of affirmation
2. Quality time

3. Receiving gifts
4. Acts of service
5. Physical touch[3]

What expressions of love mean the most to you? Which are most appreciated by your husband? Small acts of kindness in a marriage can convey special messages of love. Common courtesies, such as those we show to others outside the home, can make our homes more loving places.

Respect is also essential. Even though a man may be respected on the job, in the community, or in the church, he needs to receive respect and admiration from his wife. Respect can be demonstrated in the following ways:

1. *Speech.* We show respect for our husbands in the way we speak to them and about them. Is our correction given lovingly and beyond the hearing of others? Do we present him in a favorable light to others?
2. *Inner loveliness.* First Peter 3:3–4 encourages women to develop an inner loveliness, which the Bible describes as the "unfading beauty of a gentle and quiet spirit." It is interesting that the beauty described here is inward, rather than outward. As women, we often concentrate on clothing, makeup, body sculpting, etc., often to gain the admiration of others.
   But God is more concerned with what is inward, an attractiveness that can increase, rather than diminish, as years go by. A gentle and quiet spirit describes a wife who is at peace with her God, herself, and her calling as a wife. Such a spirit is appreciated by her husband too.
3. *A servant attitude.* In today's world, women are encouraged to claim their rights, to be more assertive, often to the point of being aggressive.

Jesus did not find it demeaning to serve others. Our attitude should be the same as His, as described in Philippians 2:5–11. He was *God*, yet He took on Himself the nature of a man, humbling Himself by coming to the earth and dying, so that every knee should bow and every tongue confess that He is Lord, to the glory of God the Father. Verse 13 of the same chapter says it is this same God who works *in us* to act according to God's pleasure and purpose. God desires to create in us the same attitude Jesus had. Galatians 5:13 also says we are to "serve one another in love." What a motto for a marriage!

4. *Self control.* Self control is an evidence of the Holy Spirit's presence in our lives. "How would I like to come home to me?" That is a question I have sometimes asked myself. When tired or stressed, many of us become irritable with those we claim to love the most. Yet we would never behave in a similar fashion with our friends or coworkers. We save our radiant smiles and tender voices for others and expect our families to understand. But, if Christ is in control of our minds and our emotions, we won't be screaming meemies (or mommies) in our homes but will give our best selves to those we love.

What's This About "Submission"?

Ephesians 5:22–24 says "Wives, submit to your husbands as to the Lord. For the husband is the head of the wife as Christ is the head of the church, his body, of which he is the Savior. Now, as the church submits to Christ, so also wives should submit to their husbands in everything." Another translation says wives are to submit to their husbands "in the same way" that Christ submitted. Christ's submissive spirit, far from being degrading, was the way in which He glorified His Father.

Submission is not a popular concept in today's me-first, do-my-own-thing environment. We seem to have a culture-wide authority problem.

When choosing a husband, a woman should consider whether he is someone to whom she will be willing to submit.

Some would say this brings to mind being a slave or a doormat, or worse, submitting to spousal abuse. But the biblical pattern has been largely misunderstood by the world and often by Christians. What we have sometimes pictured as submission is but a caricature of God's model for marriage.

The Bible balances the command for submission on the part of the wife with commands to husbands: "Husbands, love your wives, just as Christ loved the church and gave himself up for her…." (Ephesians 5:25). Christ's sacrificial, self-giving love for the church illustrates the ideal relationship. The Bible indicates that Jesus Christ was submissive to God the Father. This submission in no way made Him less God. Rather, perfect harmony typified their relationship.

Similarly, wives are not inferior to husbands but are equal with them, while serving in a supportive role of cooperation, respect, and love. Mutual submission is commanded in Ephesians 5:21, where we are all told to "submit to *one another* out of reverence for Christ." The Bible pictures a loving husband and a submissive wife but also says there is to be submission on the part of both to the Lord.

Spousal abuse is nowhere condoned in Scripture.

Love and submission characterize the Christian faith. As Christ was submissive to the Father, so the church is submissive to Christ, the wife to the husband, the children to their parents, etc. This model promotes order and harmony in the church and in the home.

The theories and practices we have substituted for God's ways are not working. Selfishness characterizes many marriages and dissension fills our homes. Children do not thrive where there is constant bickering and lack of respect. Christians frequently find themselves adopting the attitudes of the world, especially when these ideas are convincingly presented through the media. Returning to biblical principles can restore peace to our homes.

Helping Him Become a Loving Leader

Betsy wishes Mark would read the Bible and pray with her and their children. But Mark works long hours, is tired in the evening, and only wants to retreat to the newspaper and television. Prayers at tuck-in time and the task of sharing spiritual truth with their children rest solely on Betsy's shoulders, and she feels resentful.

"I never pictured our marriage this way," says Betsy. "Before we were married, Mark said he wanted a Christian home, and we planned to raise our children to know and love Christ. Now, Mark shows little interest in leading his family in spiritual areas."

Many women wish their husbands would be the loving leaders described in Ephesians 5 and 6. Some men do not realize that God expects them to be spiritual leaders in their homes. This may be due in to a lack of biblical instruction or the fact that few had fathers who set that example. Some men feel inadequate in this role and may think spirituality is for women and children only.

Sometimes a husband's attempts to lead are met with impatience and criticism from his wife. When this happens, he may become discouraged and give up, allowing his wife to become the spiritual leader in the home. A husband needs his wife's patience and respect to become all that God intended. We can pray for our husbands and encourage them as they *learn* to be spiritual leaders. Our homes should be *safe places* where it is OK to make mistakes. We are all *in process*, as God is changing us.

Does Your Husband Have a Cave?

In her teens and early twenties, Jane enjoyed slumber parties and frequent sleepovers with close girlfriends. They talked far into the night about many topics—God, their faith, their future husbands, and life in general. Jane loved those long, late-night discussions and assumed that when she married, she and her husband would share similar soul-baring times. Imagine her dismay when her beloved bridegroom did not share her love for deep discussions and late-night talks. She felt rebuffed and rejected. When her husband withdrew into his own thoughts and activities, she felt forsaken and left out of his life. Sometimes days passed with only small talk between them. What was wrong? What had she said or done to cause the distance between them?

Perhaps Jane needs to read John Gray's book, *Men are from Mars, Women are From Venus*, in order to find out about men and their "caves." I found the author helpful in defining the differing views of intimacy held by men and women. He states that women fear aloneness and men fear intimacy. Women have a great need to connect and to feel emotionally intimate. They enjoy discussing thoughts and feelings. A man's need is not as great in this area, and he may require a certain amount of "cave time."

"When a man is stressed he will withdraw into the cave of his mind and focus on solving a problem. He generally picks the most urgent problem or the most difficult. He becomes so focused on solving this one problem that he temporarily loses awareness of everything else. Other problems and responsibilities fade into the background," says Gray.

"At such times, he becomes increasingly distant, forgetful, unresponsive, and preoccupied in his relationships For example, when having a conversation with him at home, it seems as if only 5 percent of his mind is available for the relationship while the other 95 percent is still at work."[4]

Gray's counsel is that the woman not pursue but wait. Most women find this difficult. "When a man is stuck in his cave, he is powerless to give his partner the quality attention she deserves. It is hard for her to be accepting of him at these times because she doesn't know how stressed he is. If he were to come home and talk about all his problems, then she could be more compassionate. Instead he doesn't talk about his problems, and she feels he is ignoring her. She can tell he is upset but mistakenly assumes he doesn't care about her because he isn't talking to her,"[5] says Gray.

Women need to be able to share their feelings and innermost thoughts. They crave a husband's full attention when they speak, and they long to know they have been heard and understood. Disappointment results when emotional intimacy is not present in their marriages.

In his book, *Five Signs of a Loving Family*, Gary Chapman defines intimacy in this way: "The English word for intimacy comes from the Latin word *intimus*, meaning inner. Thus, intimacy involves two people opening their inner selves to each other. It is entering into each other's lives emotionally, intellectually, socially, physically, and spiritually. It is connecting at the deepest possible level in every area of life. Intimacy is accompanied by a sense of love and trust. We believe that the other person has our best interests in mind; thus, we can open ourselves up without fear that what we are telling or allowing to be seen will be used against us."[6]

Time is required to develop this depth of intimacy. It may be a lifetime quest. But it is worth praying, working, and waiting for. That's why marriage is intended to be a lifetime commitment.

Scripture Passages to Consider

- 1 Peter 3:1–7
- 1 Corinthians 7:3–5
- Ephesians 5:21–33
- Philippians 2:5–11
- Colossians 3:18–23
- Genesis 2 and 3

Things to Think About or Discuss

- What are some ways wives can express love to their husbands?
- What are some ways wives can show respect?
- Name some ways this respect can be damaged.
- Give an example of submission in marriage (preferably from your own experience).
- Many wives complain that their husbands do not talk to them. What advice would you give them?
- How can a wife encourage her husband to become a spiritual leader in their home?

CHAPTER FOUR

I'M A DAUGHTER

"You little brat!" exclaimed Valerie as she struck her eight-year-old daughter. Valerie blushed with shame as she heard the words come out of her mouth. She had become her mother! Recalling times of verbal and emotional abuse, Valerie went to God, confessing the error of her ways, reciting again the forgiveness she wanted to feel for her mother, then asking God's forgiveness for repeating the cycle. It had become an ongoing struggle. Later she apologized to her daughter.

Eleanor carries in her heart a father-hunger and struggles with bitterness because her father deserted the family when she was three years old. He was never heard from again. Sometimes she wonders if she should try to find him and dreams that he may someday return and ask her forgiveness.

None of us had perfect parents. Neither will we become perfect parents who meet every need of every child in our families. We may not understand children who are very different from ourselves, or we may be harder on children who remind us of ourselves and our past failures. We vow not to make the same mistakes our parents made, but we make them anyway or we make others. The majority of parents love their children, but they may be incapable or ignorant of showing it in ways the child can understand.

Part of becoming an adult is forgiving our parents, seeing them as fallible human beings, people we can love and respect in spite of their shortcomings. We need to sift through the teaching and examples they left us, finding what is true, biblical, and worth emulating, being willing to let go of whatever is not. This is a difficult process that often takes a lifetime.

No two children have the same parents—even in the same family. Parents change between the time the first child arrives and when later children are born. Often they gain greater wisdom. They may be more relaxed and understanding with later-born children.

What Do We "Owe" Our Parents?

We owe our parents our forgiveness, remembering that God is the only perfect parent. He can parent us throughout our entire lives, and He makes no mistakes. God can help us learn new parenting techniques and give us deeper understanding. We don't need to repeat the mistakes our parents made or become carbon copies of other members of our families. If you grew up in a dysfunctional family, be encouraged—yours can be the pivotal generation.

The Bible says we owe our parents honor (see Deuteronomy 5:16). Honoring our parents may mean providing assistance as they grow older, caring for them, assuring them of our love. Honor includes respect, courtesy, and consideration. Jesus set the example in John 19:26–27 when He lovingly entrusted the care of His mother, Mary, to the apostle John.

Our first loyalty, however, is to our spouse and the new family we are establishing. This does not imply neglect of our parents but emphasizes the priority God places on marriage.

Because people live longer today than they once did, many families find themselves in the "sandwich generation," caring for aging parents while bringing up teenagers. This situation can challenge our priorities in time, as well as in finances.

Two Families to Honor and Respect

Many a wife has exclaimed in frustration, "But, I didn't marry his family, did I?" The answer is yes, in a very real sense, you did.

With every husband comes a family—readymade—different from the one you left behind. Even if you live miles away from your husband's family, he carries in his mind the "tapes" of their history, values, and outlook. Because your thinking contains the mental tapes of your family background, you may feel that your family's way of doing things was the norm. Many disagreements within a marriage can result from differing backgrounds, whether they are economic, religious, educational, or cultural differences.

In biblical times, the husband's family frequently became a woman's primary identity. Such was the case in the Book of Ruth. Ruth and Orpah's relationship with their mother-in-law had been forged through grief and hardship.

Naomi was widowed soon after arriving in Moab, before her sons had married. Her sons married Moabite women, and after ten years Naomi's sons also died. She was comforted in her grief by the affection and faithfulness of her daughters-in-law.

Their resulting friendship was so close that Naomi's daughters-in-law wanted to leave their own country and go with her back to her native Israel. Although Naomi persuaded Orpah to return to her own people, Ruth persisted in accompanying Naomi, even to the point of claiming Naomi's God as her own.

After Ruth and Naomi arrived in Israel, Ruth continued to consult with Naomi, seek her advice, and provide for her by gleaning in the fields of Boaz. Later both Ruth and Naomi were rewarded by Ruth's marriage to Boaz and the birth of their son, Obed. Naomi found great joy and fulfillment in becoming a grandmother.

One of the greatest ways to love your husband is to love his family,

Some women, such as Marcy, have difficulty accepting a husband's family as their own.

Marcy found her husband Jim's family quiet and reserved compared to the noisy, gregarious family she had left behind several states away. While she admired their manners and orderliness, she never felt free to "let her hair down" when Jim's parents were around. She found herself criticizing them, if not aloud, at least in her own thinking. Add to that the fact that she lived away from her own family, and she missed them greatly. Jim, an only child, assumed a lot of responsibility for his aging parents. He spent a considerable amount of time in their home and usually wanted her to go along.

When Jim's mom became ill, it became Marcy's task to take her to the doctor's office once a week. Marcy worried that she would not know what to say to keep the conversation going on the long rides to a nearby city where the doctor's office was located.

On the first day she arrived to take Mom Logan to the doctor, she heard singing as she approached the house. She listened. Jim's mom was singing while accompanying herself on the piano. Not hymns but popular songs from the 50s. Marcy was surprised. In the two years since she and Jim had been married, she had not known that Mom Logan could play the piano or sing. She wondered what else she did not know about Jim's mom. It occurred to her that she had thought of Mom Logan only as Jim's mom—not as a possible friend with whom she might have something in common.

During the weekly rides to the doctor's office, Marcy learned to know her mother-in-law, to share their mutual love of music, and to enjoy her as a friend. She discovered they both enjoyed shopping and having lunch at various restaurants along the way.

Like Marcy, most of us adapted to a new family when we married. We learned that there isn't necessarily a right or wrong way of doing things, but there are differences in the way things are done. Such as, should Christmas be celebrated on Christmas Eve or Christmas morning? Are pets allowed in the house? Do we sit around the table to eat meals? Or does everyone fend for himself? Are meals served at a scheduled time? Or whenever anyone is hungry?

By focusing on what is good, couples build positive relationships and achieve a blend of the customs, beliefs, and practices of both families. In time they will also establish new traditions of their own.

Other ways we can show *love* and *respect* are:

1. Avoid criticism. By not criticizing his family, even when he does, we gain the appreciation and admiration of our spouses. Couples can help each other find what is excellent and worth emulating in both families.
2. Recognize boundaries. Parents must give wings to their married children, allowing them to establish new patterns, and recognize the new family as a separate entity.
3. Be thoughtful and considerate when making time demands. Call before dropping by. Recognize a family's need for privacy and separateness. Be available to help when needed. Celebrate special times together. Become friends, as well as family. Share the joy of grandchildren. When visits are not possible, phone calls, cards, and letters are wonderful ways to say "I'm thinking of you."

Keeping the Peace

Family feuds are stressful.

That's what Beth discovered when she married into a family with a history of discord and division. Her husband, Bill, was often cast in the role of peacemaker. Bill's brothers and sisters frequently called him to mediate their disputes, pour out their tales of woe, and get sympathy for their side of an argument.

Beth chafed when their phone calls came, and she resented the stress that Bill's family caused him. But Beth decided it was best to allow Bill to address matters of conflict within his family. She tried not to become involved or take sides. Remembering Romans 12:18, "If it is possible, as far as it depends on you, live at peace with everyone," Beth maintained good relationships with Bill's family. Although at times it has been difficult, she advises, "It's wise not to become involved in problems within your husband's family, especially issues of finance, inheritances, and similar matters. Discretion and forbearance and holding your tongue will result in fewer regrets and better relationships."

Peaceful, congenial family relationships honor the Lord and will be long remembered by our children, whereas family discord leaves bad memories and hurt feelings. We have the opportunity to model forgiveness and demonstrate biblical love within our families.

Scripture Passages to Consider

The Book of Ruth
Proverbs 3:1–2
Proverbs 10:1
Proverbs 23:22–25
Genesis 2:24
Deuteronomy 5:16
John 19:26–27
Matthew 19:4–6
Ephesians 6:2–3

Things to Think About or Discuss

- What is the promise that accompanies the commandment to honor our parents?
- Explain why you think this would be true.
- What do you admire about your husband's family?
- What are some ways you can help a new daughter-in-law or son-in-law feel a part of your family?
- How can we show honor and respect for our parents and those of our spouse?

- What is one thing you think a mother-in-law should never do?
- What are some special concerns of the sandwich generation?

TO OUR "DAUGHTERS-IN-LOVE"

For Ruthe, Stephanie, and Deborah:

When our children were small
and people commented that God had sent us only sons,
we said,
"Some people specialize!"

Later on, we said,
"We plan to let our boys get our girls!"

We trusted God to bring each of our sons the right life partner.

And He did.

Before we knew you,
when you were just a little girl,
we prayed for you.

Miles away, in places we didn't know, you grew up.

Your parents loved you, and guided you,
and you became beautiful Christian women,
just the kind we hoped our sons would choose.

Thank you for being godly mothers to our grandchildren.
As we watch you love and teach them, we join you in prayer,
that they will become men and women who follow God
all the days of their lives.

But, you are more than the mothers of our grandchildren.
You are the “daughters” we waited for, and
we love having you in our family!

____Carole Ledbetter
Mother’s Day 2002

CHAPTER FIVE

I'M A MOM (PART 1)

(This section previously published in **The Times,** *Ottawa, Illinois)*

I always wanted to be a mother. When I pushed my dolls in the small replica English pram, stuffed pieces of dry cereal into their mouths, and tucked them into their beds, I dreamed of someday having real babies of my own.

When I was ten, an admirer of the "stars of the silver screen," I wrote to movie stars such as Hedy Lamar, Lana Turner, and Rita Hayworth, requesting pictures. But, I didn't ask for glamour shots, rather pictures of them with their children. Most didn't respond, although Dale Evans sent a picture of herself with Roy and the kids.

Later, as a teenager, I prayed that someday I would be a mother. I would have other dreams—but that was the big one.

It wasn't only that I loved babies and small children. It was the *role* I was in love with. I wanted to be someone who cared, communicated, nurtured, and understood, someone who gave warmth, acceptance, and encouragement.

I was a dreamer, and motherhood was my dream.

I was an idealist too. In my high school home-management workbook, I wrote about the warm breakfasts and long tuck-in times I had planned. In my sixteen-year-old scrawl, I noted that ours would be a Christian home.

I wrote that those who wish to be mothers should seek morally strong men to be husbands and fathers—someone stable, kind, and dependable—someone who would be there and not leave when things got tough.

The man I later married has all those qualities.

But, becoming a mother didn't happen as easily as I had expected. For years we knew the pain of infertility. Five years following our marriage, after a difficult pregnancy and a Caesarean delivery, I heard the magic words, "You have a little boy!" Our son, Daniel, was born.

On two other occasions, several years apart, I would hear those words again as Paul and Timothy were added to our family.

My dream had come true. I had become the mother of three little boys.

To become a mother is to be part of a miracle.

Motherhood takes us beyond ourselves, making us responsible for the growth and development of another. It causes us to reexamine the underpinnings of our lives, to check the things we believe to be sure they are true.

Yes, there were sleepless nights, messy kitchens, dirty clothes, fights, tears, and runny noses. It wasn't always easy.

But there were bedtimes too, time for stories—the made-up ones were best (the ones we now recycle for grandchildren), time to think about God and recount the daily scuffles and scrapes that are part of little boys' lives. Time for goodnight hugs and kisses.

The years blurred like the fast-forward on the VCR. Vacations and birthdays and picnics and ball games reeled quickly by as our boys became teenagers and then grown men.

One by one, a few years apart, we delivered them to various colleges. I was excited! What did God have planned for them? Would there be "daughters" in our family someday? Would they meet them there?

Whatever else I would do in life, I knew it would be second to the task I was completing.

"No one will ever love you like your mother," said an anonymous person.

As mothers, we memorize our children. They are forever a part of us. We are always "seeing" them. Even when they are grown, we watch to see how they are doing. We admire them from a distance, trying to back off and not intrude.

We watch them parent their own children. We see what they do differently and wonder if that is where they think we failed. It is their turn now.

I was a stoic, first child. When I was in the seventh grade, a friend and I were riding double on my bicycle. (A hundred years ago, riding double and chewing gum were major school offenses.) My friend and I crashed into the curb while trying to escape the teasing of several eighth-grade boys. My friend was bleeding; her teeth had been knocked loose. Everyone crowded around her, especially the teachers, who reminded us that we shouldn't have been riding double.

My left arm wouldn't move, but no one noticed. With my right hand I guided the bicycle toward home. I didn't cry, because there was no one to care. Why waste tears? But when I saw my mother, the tears came. I have always remembered waiting to cry because I wanted my mother to be there when I did. Mothers absorb our tears and their soft, warm arms encircle our grief. In a mother's arms, the world turns right side up again.

I understand that not all women find fulfillment in motherhood. Most women have multiple roles and other dreams they want to pursue. In many cases today, being a mother seems to be incidental to all the other things going on in a woman's life.

I am sad for women who see motherhood as an accident and their children as an inconvenience. Because, from my point of view, it will always be the most fulfilling thing I have ever done.

Being a Mom Changes Us

In the last fifty years, we have heard a lot of about feminism and women's rights to equality. But some women feel the feminist movement has cheated them by downplaying motherhood. Many women have turned away from the feminist movement that encouraged them to be smart and successful because it also encouraged them to be hostile and demeaning to men.

When you become a parent, your own interests become secondary to the needs of your children. You grow up, forget about obsessing about your appearance, and begin to focus your energies on trying to raise healthy boys and girls who will grow up to be good and successful men and women.

"Motherhood opens a new world of conflicting emotions,"[1] says author Nancy Ortberg, in her article, "The Jekyll and Hyde of Motherhood."

"Two different people emerged when I became a mother," says Nancy. "God uses the tensions of motherhood to shatter our illusions…God uses motherhood to show us we need him…to reveal his character."

Parenting offers opportunities to grow in ways we never expected.

I asked the women in my Sunday morning Bible class what changes motherhood brought in their lives. They replied: "Motherhood brought contentment to my life—filled an empty space in me." "Made me realize how unprepared I was to raise a child." "I was amazed at the love I had for my baby." "It took the focus off of my needs, wants, and concerns and placed it on the baby." "I became less willing to take risks." "It grew me up. My thinking became less self-centered and more aware of my example." "I learned that the only lasting legacy we can pass on to our children is not material but spiritual."

God Loves Kids

"There's no greater calling than to be a responsible mother or father to our children," says author, Emilie Barnes. "We desperately need good parents for the children God has given us. Before the foundation of this earth, our children were planned just for us. We must believe and continue as best we know how to raise and prepare our children for God's calling—whatever and wherever that may be."[2]

Jesus spoke tenderly concerning little children in Mark 10:14: "Let the little children come to me, do not hinder them, for the kingdom of God belongs to such as these." Children were greatly valued in biblical times. Today newspaper headlines tell us children are often unwanted, neglected, and abused. They are frequently looked upon as an inconvenience and an interruption to our plans for self-fulfillment. But, our children are eternal beings, gifts from God to be nurtured and reborn into His kingdom.

Jesus said a little child is the "greatest in the kingdom of Heaven," and He taught His disciples that unless they were changed and became like children, they could not enter that kingdom. Psalm 127:3 says, "Sons are a heritage from the Lord, children a reward from him"; and Psalm 113:9 describes a "happy mother of children." A happy mother is a great gift!

Each time I became pregnant I felt I was on a great adventure with God. And I didn't have to do anything to help the process except to get the proper rest and nutrition. It was all in God's hands and under His control. God was performing a miracle within me.

When our first son was born, we received a note from our doctor congratulating us and telling us we would enjoy this child for the rest of our lives. I have found no other role so fulfilling as that of being a wife and mother. My husband and I look forward to enjoying each of our children and grandchildren for all eternity

Why isn't parenting looked upon today as the divine privilege it once was? Perhaps because it's seen to be a very difficult, if not impossible, task. People fear not doing it right or think only of the inconvenience and expense children bring. Yes, children are inconvenient, messy, noisy, sometimes troublesome, and expensive—but still wonderful. Because people are eternal. Someone said, "In the end, all that matters is God and people." No wonder Jesus stressed the importance of children and often used them as illustrations in His sermons.

Parenting Is an Important and Challenging Job

Unfortunately, not long after the birth of a new baby, it is not unusual for parents to feel tired, helpless, and frustrated. The wonder of this tiny new person is lost in the drudgery of 2:00 A.M. feedings and endless diaper changes.

The teaching and nurturing process necessary to create a responsible adult will take at least eighteen years, and there will be many times of struggle and discouragement as well as joy and celebration.

Where Is Help?

First of all, we can depend upon God and our personal day-by-day walk with Him, leaning on Him and looking to His Word for guidance and instruction. Often grandmothers, aunts, sisters, and other family members can help too. It's time to be teachable. But whose advice should we heed? While many excellent parenting books are on the market, not all of them agree. Books can be helpful, but parents need to be convinced that they are adequate for the task and that their "sanctified common sense" is reliable.

People today find parenting more difficult than other generations did for a number of reasons. One of these is the number of "experts" in the field. There are more books available today on parenting than ever before. Many of these books are helpful, but the record number of sales highlights the fact that most people still feel inadequate as parents. Parents today fear their children. They are afraid of the "terrible twos" and the "turbulent teens." Our limited knowledge of psychology, coming from newspaper, magazines, etc., makes us think we cannot raise our children without somehow damaging them in the process.

Most studies focus on the behavior of the child rather than the behavior of the parent. But for Christian parents, the evidence of the Holy Spirit's working in a parent's life, producing the fruit mentioned in Galatians 5:22, 23, will do more to influence children in the right direction than all of the advice on child training. Our children will absorb the attitudes and atmosphere of our homes. If our homes are peaceful, happy, orderly places where God and His Word are honored on a day-to-day basis, our children will find it easier to follow the pattern. Even babies can sense discord and tension.

Don't Forget Daddy

Fathers sometimes feel left out in the months following the arrival of a new baby. As women, we may find it difficult to balance our various roles and give adequate time and attention to our husbands, feeling overwhelmed by the responsibilities of being a mother. It may appear to the husband that everything revolves around the baby.

Wives appreciate husbands who understand and show patience during these times.

When the new baby settles into more of a predictable routine, a woman can return her attention to the marriage relationship, making sure it remains strong and stable. I recently read this poignant statement made by a woman expressing regret over the failure of her marriage. She said, "He wanted a wife and I became a mother."

Unfortunately, after the arrival of children, a woman may begin to draw her emotional support primarily from her children, as her husband increasingly looks to his job for personal satisfaction. But the marriage must remain the first priority.

The children reflect the marriage.

As the mother of three sons, I remember reminding myself that I would someday give each of our sons away, but their dad would be the one I would get to keep. The child who grows up witnessing the love and commitment of his parents to God and to each other receives a precious lifetime gift.

What About Big Brother (or Sister)?

Older children need to be reassured that the new baby has not taken their place. Upon arriving home with our third son, I placed him in his crib to continue sleeping while I gave my attention to our two older boys. I thought this was important because my children were born at a time when a Caesarean section required being in the hospital for a week to ten days. That's a long time to be away from your children.

I continued to spend special times with each child on a daily basis while the youngest was sleeping.

When babies become toddlers, older children appreciate places to keep their toys and belongings where younger siblings can't destroy them. While sharing should be encouraged, an older child's privacy should also be respected.

Each new baby is a special gift, an individual not like any other ever created, a treasure to be cherished, a life to be molded and shaped according to the plan of an eternal God.

Scripture Passages to Consider

- Matthew 18:2-6
- Matthew 19:13-14
- Mark 10:13-16
- Psalm 8:2a

Things to Think About or Discuss

- How did becoming a mother change you?
- What was the greatest frustration you faced when your children were small?
- How did others help you?
- How could they have helped more?

- What steps can at-home moms take to stay in touch with the adult world?
- If you are a mom who works outside your home, give some tips working moms could use.
- How can a new father be made to feel included and not shut out?
- What is the best way for mothers, mothers-in-law, grandmothers, etc. to help when a new baby arrives?
- How can the church help?
- What would you like to say to a new mom?

CHAPTER SIX

I'M A MOM (PART 2)

We remember some days, not because a great event took place, but because they remind us of the turning of life's pages, like the shifting of particles in a kaleidoscope, causing us to view things in a new way.

I remember such a day in June 1982. Our oldest son had recently completed his first year of college in a neighboring state. We traveled as a family to a wedding in southern Illinois. It was good to be together again—all five of us, my husband and I, and three long-legged sons, packed into our 1979 Chevy Impala.

At the wedding reception, I stood back and observed our three sons as they mingled with the guests. Perhaps for the first time, I saw them, not as little boys, but as young men approaching the threshold of manhood. An attractive young lady invited our middle son to dance. With poise he accepted and I watched them move across the dance floor. I noticed our oldest son engaged in conversation with adult members of the family. Even our youngest—approaching twelve—appeared more grownup and mature than I had previously noticed.

I felt joy…and a sense of anticipation.

A few days after returning home, I read John, chapter 17, where Jesus was preparing to leave His beloved disciples, sending them out into the world, after which He would return to the Father. I wondered if Jesus had experienced the same feelings concerning His disciples as I felt regarding our sons' approaching manhood. I read more closely Jesus' prayer for those He loved. He said, "I do not ask that you take them out of the world, but that you keep them from the evil one" (John 17:15). It was verse 19 that gripped me: "For them I sanctify myself, that they too may be truly sanctified." Jesus' example was the greatest part of His teaching. He had taught them the truth of His word (vs. 14), prayed for them (vs. 15), kept them. Now He sent them into the world (verse 18) and turned to follow the Father's path for Himself: to face the cross, anticipating the resurrection and His Father's face.

Similarly, in preparing our children for whatever God has for them, our example is the greatest part of our teaching. We must sanctify *ourselves*. We must follow the God we teach them about.

What the Bible has to say about parenting can be summed up as

- teaching and training our children,
- modeling the behavior we want to see in them, and
- providing unconditional love.

Train Up a Child

I don't consider myself an authority on teaching and training children. I have received help from many sources, not the least of which has been from authors such as Ross Campbell, Anna Mow, Gary Smalley, and John Trent, from whom I quote in this chapter.

While example remains our most effective tool in training our children, example without relationship will fall short of the desired result. Unless your child feels secure in your love, he will not respond to your teaching and training in the way you desire. Most parents *do* love their children, but many children do not *feel* truly loved in an unconditional way. Why not?

"Although love is within the heart of almost all parents, the challenge is to convey this love to their child,"[1] says Ross Campbell in his book, *How to Really Love Your Child.*

Ways suggested by Ross Campbell to convey love to a child include the importance of eye contact, physical touch, and focused attention. In his lecture series on parent/child relationships, he states that he spends three or four hours talking about how to love a child before discussing discipline. He believes parents have separated love from discipline as if they were two separate entities. "The first fact we must understand in order to have a well-disciplined child is that making a child feel loved is the first and most important part of good discipline. Of course, this is not all, but it is most important....

"In the realm of child rearing, discipline is *training* a child in mind and character to enable him to become a self-controlled, constructive member of society. What does this involve? Discipline involves training through every type of communication. Guidance by example, modeling, verbal instruction, written instruction, verbal requests, written requests, teaching, providing learning and fun experiences....

"*Discipline is immeasurably easier when the child feels genuinely loved.* This is because he wants to identify with the parents, and is able to do so only if he knows he is truly loved and accepted. He is then able to accept his parents' guidance without hostility and obstructiveness."[2]

Discipline Includes Correction

"Train a child in the way he should go, and when he is old he will not turn from it." This quote from Proverbs 22:6 has been the consolation to many a parent.

In my early years of parenting, I did not find much comfort in the thought that my children might sow their wild oats, make their lives a thicket of complications, and then one day in old age return to their earlier faith in Christ. Now I know that is *not* what the verse means. *Old* simply indicates "when they are grown," not necessarily in advanced age.

One of the important emphases in this verse is that a child needs to be trained in the way *he* should go, indicating that all children are not alike. This verse in the Berkeley Version of the Bible reads: "Educate a child according to his life requirements; even when he is old he will not veer from it." Children need to be trained, educated, and nurtured with a view to the development of their character, not simply "punished into shape" so that they can rebel at a later time.

Proverbs 13:24 speaks of the rod of correction: "He who spares the rod hates his son, but he who loves him is careful to discipline him." While some have used this verse to excuse harshness, cruelty, and child abuse, the emphasis of the command is on correction, or training, not punishment for its own sake. Studies indicate troubled young people frequently come from punitive homes where harsh discipline is administered and little love is shown.

God sometimes chastens us as His children in ways that are painful but instructive. In Psalm 89:32–33 He says to Israel: "I will punish their sin with the rod, their iniquity with flogging, but I will not take my love from him, nor will I ever betray my faithfulness."

Because of our fallenness, we sometimes chasten our children out of frustration and anger rather than out of love and self-discipline. Our heavenly Father does not do this. While our methods may vary, God holds us responsible to observe our children's behavior and provide correction in an appropriate manner.

Modeling Behavior through Our Response to God

It's not primarily what you *do,* it's how you *are* that counts. While correction often receives the greatest amount of attention in books and magazines, the most important part of child training involves a natural kind of modeling and sharing, such as that portrayed in Deuteronomy 6:4–9. Parents were expected to love God and His commandments before trying to impress them upon their children. Then the teaching in the home could take place in the course of daily living. If parents view God's commandments as good and wholesome, children will be less likely to have authority problems or to see God's rules as legalism.

I love Anna Mow's book, *Your Child From Birth to Rebirth.* It's an old book, but of all the books on parenting that I have read in my lifetime it is the one that helped me the most. In it she reiterates the following three points from Deuteronomy 6:4-9:

> The Israelites first expected the *parents to be whole in their own response to God* (vv. 4, 5). This is the basic teaching method, the greatest method of all—the *living* of the truth. Even then they saw that this was the basic

> learning method of every child. There is no substitute for the *unconscious teaching* which communicates what we are long before any teaching can be communicated by words. When the child finally learns the words he will be able to say, "Oh, yes, I knew that long ago."
>
> Then those people of ancient times saw the importance of the *informal teaching* parents were doing every day (vv 6, 7). This method also outweighs and undergirds all formal teaching. This is learning for all of life, not just during special hours: when sitting at home, while going for a walk, when going to bed, and when getting up in the morning...In other words, parents should talk about God as naturally as they talk about food and clothes. This suits the understanding of a child because to him there is no distinction between the secular and the sacred. In this the child is more Christlike than adults are, for God belongs in all of life.
>
> The third method emphasized for religious education in the home in early Jewish history was by *visual methods*...their visual religious education included house decorating (vv. 8, 9) and symbols to be worn, as well as rituals to be performed. Even their rituals were to be performed in the home where the children were. Their purpose in all these methods was to create curiosity of motivation in the child so that he would ask the questions about God that the parents hoped he would ask. "When, in time to come, your son asks you, 'What is the meaning of these things?' you shall tell him, 'Before our eyes...God helped us'" (Deuteronomy 6:20, 21). They knew that God not only *made* their environment, He wanted to *be* their environment.[3]

You may have heard it said that, "God has no grandchildren," indicating that every individual must come to personal faith in Christ and cannot depend on the beliefs of others. So it is with our children.

With regard to the conversion of children, Anna says, "We need deeper meanings of conversion, which is more *to* Someone than from some condition. If we have emphasized a certain kind of emotional experience as conversion, rather than establishing a living relationship with Christ which grows in daily experience, then we have caused many to stumble as they try to hold a certain 'feeling' they once had. This new relationship with God is more faith than feeling.[4]

"The religion that Jesus revealed by His life and teaching required the *giving* of one's *whole life* to God in a new personal relationship. Dependence upon ritual performance and good deeds can become a religious substitute and can actually separate one from God if the *whole life* is not given to Him.

"Mere obedience is no guarantee of character. The *reason* for the obedience is the determining factor. This capacity for choice in obedience must develop and grow even after one is a Christian."[5]

Bless Your Children

We all long to be accepted by others. While we may say "I don't care what other people think" on the inside we yearn for intimacy and affection. Children desperately desire their parents' approval. We are shaped by those who love us, as well as those who withhold their love. Even after we are grown we desire the approval of our parents. When they are no longer living we still think about how they would regard us if they were alive. Enjoying or missing out on our parents' approval has a lifelong effect upon us, affecting also our relationships with others: spouse, friends, co-workers, and children.

In their book, *The Blessing,* Gary Smalley and John Trent state:

> For sons or daughters in biblical times, receiving their father's blessing was a momentous event...it gave these children a tremendous sense of being highly valued by their parents and even pictured a special future for them. At a specific point in their lives they would hear words of encouragement, love, and acceptance from their parents...In Old Testament times, this blessing was primarily reserved for one special occasion. In contrast, parents today can decide to build these elements of blessing into their children's lives daily."[6]

Genesis 27 recounts the story of Jacob and Esau and the stolen blessing. Esau is devastated at the realization that he had lost his father's blessing to his conniving brother. Verse 38 echoes his despair: "'Do you have only one blessing, my father? Bless me too, my father!' Then Esau wept aloud."

Ways to express our acceptance and bless our children listed by Smalley and Trent in *The Blessing* include

- meaningful touch
- spoken words
- expressing high value
- picturing a special future
- an active commitment[7]

Discussing the power of spoken words, Smalley and Trent state: "Words have incredible power to build us up or tear us down emotionally. This is particularly true when it comes to giving or gaining family approval. Many people can clearly remember words of praise their parents spoke years ago. Others can remember negative words they heard—and what their parents were wearing when they spoke them!

"Throughout the Scriptures, we find a keen recognition of the power and importance of spoken words. In the very beginning, God 'spoke' and the world came into being (Genesis 1:3)."[8]

In Genesis 48 and 49, Jacob pronounced a blessing for each of his twelve sons and two of his grandchildren. After he had finished blessing each child, the Bible states: "this is what their father (Jacob) said to them; when he blessed them. He blessed them, *every one*, with the blessing appropriate to him" (Genesis 49:28 NASB).

We must talk to our children and our words need to provide the encouragement and affirmation for which they hunger.

Scripture Passages Further Study and Discussion

- Proverbs 22:15
- Proverbs 29:15
- Hebrews 12:4–12
- 1 Samuel 3:11–14

Things to Think About or Discuss

- Do you see a difference between instruction and training? (See Ephesians 6:4.)
- Ephesians 6:4 speaks of "exasperating" our children. How might a parent do that?
- What does it mean to "bless" your children? How did your parents bless you?
- Suggest some ways to help children feel loved and accepted.
- How can you accept a child whose behavior is unacceptable?
- How can we teach our children the meaning of grace in our dealings with them?

CHAPTER SEVEN

I'M A HOMEMAKER

Because I used to work in a home interiors store, I can tell you that people's homes are important to them. Whether a single room or a sprawling mansion, people give much thought and spend great amounts of money on the places they call home. Many songs have been written, fondly recalling the joys of this place called home. Home means comfort, a place where you belong, somewhere to rest at the end of a day or a journey. Home is where we are most ourselves. Or, as someone has said, "Home is where they have to let you in."

What a privilege for women to be called in Titus 2 (KJV) "keepers of the home." While the responsibility for the keeping of the home can be shared by all who live there, as women, we are the ones who set the emotional tone.

What sort of homes does God expect us to keep?

Orderly Homes

What does it mean to be organized? A partial definition from the *Webster's New World College Dictionary, Fourth*

Edition, Copyright 1999 by Macmillan USA says in part, "to arrange in an orderly way…"[1] It means we have a plan for creating an orderly home where our loved ones feel safe, relaxed, and able to develop to their full potential.

First Corinthians 14:40 (NASB) says, "Everything should be done in a fitting and orderly way."

Emilie Barnes, in her book, *Emilie's Creative Home Organizer*, states: "Being a homemaker, full-time or part-time, is a gift. Every woman should realize that she has the greatest profession in the whole wide world.

"How you organize your home and life will determine how effective and efficient you are in this honorable position….

"Recently, I saw a sign which read: 'I had my home clean last week; I'm sorry you missed it.' Even though most of us would like a clean, orderly home because it brings pleasure and peace of mind, we must remember that most homemakers have never had their home in perfect order….

"Organization begins now,"[2] says Emilie.

Most of us need to heed Emilie's instruction to get organized, go through our "stuff" and either put it away, throw it away, or give it away. I am always amazed how good I feel after cleaning my closets and getting rid of the things I no longer need or want.

Home management involves time management and, those much-dreaded words, *self discipline*. Since I have difficulty focusing on one task at a time, this is an area where I need to grow.

Time management requires me to ask, "What am I trying to do with my life?" "What are my goals?" "What does God want me to do?"

When I feel stressed, I need to ask, "What am I doing that is not part of His plan?" "What am I doing in order to 'look good' in the eyes of others?"

It may be that I may need to weed out the clutter in my life as well as my closets.

Gracious Homes

I enjoy looking at magazines with pictures of beautiful homes. Sometimes they are called "gracious" homes. Is your home gracious? Is mine? Can a home be called gracious? Or could that only refer to the people who live there?

Sometimes those of us who extol the grace of God are the least gracious to the people in our own homes. Take the "milk test" to check the tension level in your home. Suppose one of your children upsets his glass of milk at the dinner table. What happens? How gracious are we to those who make mistakes or cause us inconvenience and extra work? Are we forgiving when our spouse forgets to get or do something we requested? While there are many things we can do to add a gracious touch to our homes, the most important is to display the fruit of the Holy Spirit in our actions and reactions.

Besides being gracious people, other suggestions to make our homes hospitable and welcoming might include special touches, such as lighting candles (during a meal or anytime), playing relaxing music, fresh flowers, turning off the TV and reading aloud as a family, sharing a serendipity (something unexpectedly nice that happened during your day), developing family games and rituals, asking "How can I pray for you today?" These little extras bind us together and provide our children with lasting memories.

My friend, Marcia, whom I hadn't seen for a long time, called one day and said, "When I come to your house, could you serve me coffee in one of your China cups like you used to do?" I was amazed that she remembered such a small detail. I often use mugs, but she remembered the times I had used the China cups Actually, it takes no longer to wash a China cup than it does a ceramic mug.

I would vote to bring back the family dinner table where everyone gathered daily to share hot food and the events of the day. Does anyone mourn its loss? For many families in the past it was a time to build family traditions, relate truth, and discuss a myriad of topics. Some families prayed together and read the Bible after the meal.

Perhaps families today accomplish these things in other ways, at other times. Or are we too busy, with everyone going in different directions? What would we have to sacrifice to do it?

Hospitable Homes

Are you waiting for your home to be perfect before opening your door to guests? If so, that day will never come. And, if our homes are absolutely perfect, our guests may not feel at home there. The Bible encourages us to show hospitality, which is different from entertaining. Few of us are entertainers, but all of us can share what we have, whether a simple meal or a bowl of popcorn, with others. Dinner table conversations with people of various ages and walks of life not only enrich our life experience but provide a memorable gift to our children. Inviting a visiting missionary or a family new in the neighborhood over for dinner can be an adventure for the whole family.

What Would I Do All Day?

"I would go crazy if I were at home all the time," a young woman recently remarked. With all of the labor-saving devices available today, is there enough for a woman to do at home? Would the apostle Paul, if he were writing today, tell women to be "busy at home"? Or, would he suggest they find careers elsewhere?

Some women count it a privilege to be full-time homemakers while others, from economic necessity or the desire to pursue a career, feel they must also work outside the home.

Louise Story in the *New York Times*, September 20, 2005, says: "Many women at the nation's most elite colleges say they have already decided that they will put aside their careers in favor of raising children. Though some of these students are not planning to have children, and some hope to have a family and work full time, many others say they will happily play a traditional female role, with motherhood their main commitment."[3]

Whether full-time or part-time, being a homemaker remains a challenging and important task. There is still much to do—keeping our homes clean and orderly (not perfect), meals prepared with love and forethought, groceries stocked, financial records kept, children loved and taught—the list is long.

Many homemakers find time for more personal things too: crafts, decorating, sewing, volunteer work, reading, walking, praying, studying God's Word, perhaps even a home business.

Although most of us feel inadequate when comparing ourselves with the woman described in Proverbs 31, she certainly found plenty to do! What impresses me most is her vigor and enthusiasm. Verse 27 summarizes her well: "She watches over the affairs of her household and does not eat the bread of idleness."

We all have a limited amount of time and energy.

Choices must be made as to how we spend our lives. We can ask God to "Teach us to number our days aright, that we may gain a heart of wisdom" (Psalm 90:12). Or we can simply be bumped along by whatever comes next, with no particular plan in mind.

Godly Homes

What makes a godly home? Is it simply that the people who live there go to church on Sunday? Or recite a certain creed? Or is it whether the people who live there behave in a Christian manner in their homes? I believe it depends on where our home is centered. Is it centered in the children? The church? The TV? Friends? Activities? Possessions? Or is it our purpose to honor Christ and live out His plan for us? If this is our desire, it will be evident in our conversation, entertainment, activities, and goals.

We need to echo Joshua's resolve: "As for me and my household, we will serve the Lord." (Joshua 24:15b)

(If you are using this book in a group setting, share organizational ideas, household or time management tips.)

THE DINNER TABLE'S DEMISE

When did we stop eating together? Around tables set with delicious, hot food.

When did cookbooks become collector's items? Not spotted and worn like Grandma's.

When did we stop talking over heaping plates of succulent morsels?

The days when six o'clock brought wonderful aromas of home-cooked meals

Are forgotten in today's rushed lifestyles.

Why did the dinner table die?

Was there an inquest?

Was it television that made us a nation of "grazers" and take-out junkies?

The hectic pace of long hours, shift work, Mom's job, Dad's job, convenience food?

Individualism—everyone hurrying to do his own thing?

Two or three cars shuttling people to their various activities.

Was it the fitness craze?

Food is bad for you, you know.

Was it our avid interest in sports? (Is there *always* a game going on?)

What have we lost? Who cares? Were there any mourners?

Perhaps we should mourn the loss of

- Connection: sharing each other's lives, telling of the day's events.
- Closeness: praying together, caring for one another.

- Cooperation: making and taking time to be together.
- Conversation: it's an art, the trading of information, thoughts, and feelings.
- Cohesiveness: the feeling of being a family, not separate individuals.
- Culinary delights: served hot. Recipes passed down for generations.
- Culture: manners, family traditions, values.
- Christian teaching: Dad, what does the Bible say about that?
- Can we accomplish these things in other ways, at other times?

Perhaps.

But will we? What better time and place than at the family dinner table?

What would it cost us to bring it back?

Effort, convenience, planning, revised priorities?

What will it cost us if we don't?

___Carole Ledbetter
1999

CHAPTER EIGHT

I'M A GRANDMOTHER

AUGUST 13, 1991

Hello, Grandma!" said my husband.

I sat at my desk in the bank where I worked when Don called. The greatly anticipated day had come: I was a grandmother—to identical twin girls, Emily and Sarah. We hurried to Lutheran General Hospital in Park Ridge to rejoice with Dan and Ruthe at the birth of their daughters. We were grandparents.

From our first jaunt to the preemie ward to their fifteenth birthday party last August, it has been an adventure. There were four more happy phone calls over the space of the next ten years: four more grandchildren—two girls and two boys—Ashley, Collin, Lauren, and Carson.

Some of the calls came in the middle of the night.

"Showtime!" exclaimed our son, Paul, calling at 2:00 A.M. on July 15, 2001. I was invited to come to Kankakee, Illinois to witness the birth of our youngest grandson, Carson Paul. But I decided to wait until morning, and by the time my husband, Don, and I arrived, the baby had been born. What a wonderful little boy he is!

What is the role of a grandmother in the twenty-first century?

We are experiencing a time of great diversity; there are all kinds of grandmothers today. Some are called by traditional titles, such as grandmother, or grandma, or granny—others have fancier names, such as Granbie, Meemaw, or Gee Gee. Few grandmothers sit on the porch and knit as they are sometimes pictured (although some may knit beside a swimming pool in Florida in the winter). Grandma can be found at the fitness center, the YMCA, or the local junior college. Maybe she works at Wal-Mart. She may travel to distant parts of the globe. Many grandmothers provide child care, and today greater numbers are raising their grandchildren, becoming the principal caregiver, while some live far away from their grandchildren and may see them once a year or less. Grandma has to hop a plane!

Grandma doesn't look like she used to either. As I view ancient pictures of my grandmothers I notice their hairstyles were very different than those of today, their fashions decidedly "old" in comparison to the way many stylish grandmas currently dress.

Grandmothers may be young or old, fat or thin, grumpy or gracious, fun or fastidious!

But grandmothering is a privilege. (When did it become a verb?)

When my turn came, I wanted to make the most of it!

What does God want a grandmother to do? (Or not do?) Again those verses from Titus 2:3–5 came to mind: "Likewise, teach the older women to be reverent in the way they live, not to be slanderers or addicted to much wine, but to teach what is good. Then they can train the younger women to love their husbands and children, to be self-controlled and pure, to be busy at home, to be kind, and to be subject to their husbands, so that no one will malign the Word of God."

The words may sound a bit old-fashioned in today's world, but the principles remain good advice.

Reverence, positive speech, temperance, goodness, and love become the qualities we should exemplify as mature women. By setting an example, grandmothers can teach younger women to love their families, stay emotionally balanced and pure, maintain their homes, and honor their husbands, so that God's people will have a good reputation before a confused world that needs to see that God's ways really do work.

In the Bible, Timothy's grandmother, Lois, as well as his mother, Eunice, is credited with imparting a sincere faith to young Timothy (2 Timothy 1:5).

Grandmothers can influence generations still unborn.

These are some of the things we can do.

Pray

A godly grandmother can make a difference in the life of her grandchildren by praying they will come to faith in Christ at an early age, that they will grow up with the ability to make good choices, to say no to what is wrong and an enthusiastic yes to God's plan in their lives.

Our own calm and peaceful lives can be a stabilizing influence. Children need to observe adults who trust God, love each other, and don't fall apart at every event in life. We demonstrate with our lives what it means to follow Christ.

We can teach our grandchildren to pray by praying with them. When they visit your home, you can pray with them at bedtime or before meals. When they are troubled or have a problem, you can suggest, "Let's tell God about it!" We can teach them to praise God by occasionally saying, "Let's thank God for the good time we had today!"

Don't force the child to pray. If you pray simply and spontaneously, the child will feel free to add his prayers to yours. Your grandchild will remember that praying is what you do when you are joyful or troubled.

Play

It's time to play! To reawaken your imagination! A grandmother should be a fun person. Playing with your grandchildren is a great way to relate to them. You can play board games or make believe. We should never grow too old to play, and our grandchildren can provide opportunities for us to be children again.

Last fall, my granddaughter, Ashley, and I slept in the playhouse in the woods behind her home. We built a fire and roasted marshmallows. Then we read and talked until we were sleepy. All of the air leaked out of the air mattress before morning and my shoulders ached from the pressure of the wooden floor boards. But I wouldn't have missed the experience. In the morning we prepared a breakfast of weeds and leaves and berries and pretended to eat them. Then, after a hike in the woods behind the playhouse, climbing over logs, and jumping the creek, we set off for a real breakfast at a local restaurant.

Over the past ten years, I have become a puddle walker, bicycle rider, hiker, the "adoption lady" who brings the new baby (doll), the "doctor" who delivers the baby, the "nurse" who helps care for the baby, the mother of countless dolls, the saleslady at the store, and numerous other pretend characters. I have welcomed messy kitchens as we cut out Christmas cookies and visited local pet stores until

I became well acquainted with the owner. And now that we have teenagers, I have an excuse to go shopping in the teen section. My husband, a champion Chinese Checker player, has instructed the grandchildren on how to beat Grandma every time. These are just some of the joys of grandparenting!

Read and share stories

"Never miss a chance to read a child a story," says Max Lucado. Stories are one of the best ways to grow close to grandchildren. They are so much better than TV, because the child must form the pictures in his mind, which encourages imagination. Some stories can be true, stories of long ago, your life stories and those of members of your family. Children need to know the stories of the people who have gone before them. Share your own story of how you came to personal faith in Christ, and times when He answered your prayers. Talk to your grandchildren about God in a relaxed non-scolding way. Don't preach or shame them but emphasize God's love and His wonderful plan for their lives.

Ashley loves to hear stories about when her daddy was a little boy. When something out of the ordinary happened at their house, she used to say to me, "Guess what your little boy did today!"

Grandmothers can introduce a love for good literature and encourage imagination by their choice of books. The library is a wonderful resource!

Taking trips with grandchildren can also be a point of contact. Even local sites can be entertaining; Collin, Lauren, and Carson like to visit the local parks and the pet store.

If your grandchildren live far away, you can write letters. My Aunt Eleda wrote to each of her grandchildren regularly until she was ninety-three years old. What a treasure those letters must be now that she is gone!

Another woman I know sends "grandma boxes" to her grandchildren who live far away. She collects novelty items and small gifts over a couple months, packages them, and mails them. Occasionally, when she forgets, one of her grandchildren will ask, "Isn't it about time for a "grandma box?"

The Bible speaks of our "children's children" and makes promises to those who follow God. If we follow the Lord, living out His purpose in our lives, we can expect He will work in the lives of those who follow after us.

Scripture Passages to Consider

- Proverbs 13:22
- Proverbs 17:6
- Psalm 103:17
- Ezekiel 37:25
- Psalm 128:6

Things to Think About or Discuss

- What is one thing your grandmother taught you?
- How did your grandmother influence your Christian faith?
- What is your best memory of your grandmother?
- What advice would you like to give to your granddaughter?

CHAPTER NINE

I'M A FRIEND

I still remember my first best friend. Her name was Nona and we met in the first grade.

She had light brown hair, a shy smile, and glasses that accentuated her beautiful green eyes. One sunny afternoon in the early fall, after going home to eat lunch (children did that in those days), we walked back to school, dawdling along, stopping at the candy store for penny candy, and then when we were several blocks away from school, we heard the clang of the school bell signaling we were tardy! Because we had never been late before, we were afraid to go to school. We might have to go to the principal's office and we didn't know what happened to children who went there. We were sure it wasn't something good, so we decided to play hooky and spent the afternoon running through backyards, hiding from the truant officer, convinced he would be out looking for us. But alas, we went home too soon and wound up having to confess to our parents that we didn't go to school at all that afternoon.

Nona confessed to her mother immediately, but I held my silence—until Nona finally told my mother too. Fortunately, I had a gracious mother who didn't fear I would become a confirmed truant.

I've had many friends in the years that followed, friends with whom I giggled, played, prayed, and dreamed, as a teenager and as a young adult. I recall friends with whom my husband and I shared the child-rearing years—couples we knew and grew to love—with whom we still keep in touch. Now most of my friends are grandmothers like me, and we are growing older, although we hate to admit it. I am continually making new friends too, friends of all ages. When our children were growing up, their friends were also mine. I love receiving Christmas greetings from them. I need people of all ages in my life.

Friendship Is a Gift

We inherit our relatives, but we choose our friends.

If you have had several close friendships over a lifetime, consider yourself blessed. Most of us will have many acquaintances but only a few friends.

The Bible has a number of things to say about friendship, among them: "A friend loves at all times" (Proverbs 17:17); a friend is honest: "Wounds from a friend can be trusted, but an enemy multiplies kisses" (Proverbs 27:6). We should not forsake a friend or a friend of our parent (Proverbs 27:10).

These are only a few; there are many more references to friendship in the Bible.

This past summer, on a trip to San Antonio, Texas, I spent time with my friend, Ruth, who was my best friend at the giggly age of twelve and on through high school. Over lunch at a swanky restaurant, we picked up our friendship right where we left off forty years ago.

The friends I have made are "forever friends," and I consider them gifts from a loving God. I remember reading that "All the love we receive in a lifetime comes from God," so I thank Him for the love I have received from friends.

Friends of God

In the Bible, Abraham is called a "friend of God." God spoke to him to tell him to leave his country and move to a place Abraham had never seen. God told Abraham he would become the father of a great nation and through him all nations of the earth would be blessed. Abraham trusted God and demonstrated his faith through obedience. (Genesis 12:1-4, 2 Chronicles 20:7 and James 2:23)

Moses is also called a friend of God, someone with whom God spoke face to face, as friends do. "The Lord would speak to Moses face to face, as a man speaks with his friend," says Exodus 33:11.

In each instance God initiated the relationship. There was no merit on the part of the one chosen, but both Abraham and Moses responded in trust and obedience. Trust is what enables people to be friends, and, in the case of Abraham and Moses, trust produced obedience.

Jesus, the Best Friend of All

Trusting Jesus makes God my friend.

"Christ did not lay down his life for us as enemies so that we should remain enemies, but so that he could make us friends," said Thomas Aquinas, in his *Lectures on the Gospel of John*.

Jesus came into the world over two thousand years ago so that we might become His friends. You and I, and all others who respond to His call, can actually become friends of Jesus! John 1:12 says that those who receive Him, believing on His name, become His children. He came not only to save us from our sins but so that we could become His friends.

In John chapter 15, verses 12–17, Jesus tells us we must love His other children, and that if we are truly His friends, we will do this. He says we are not His servants but His friends. Just as true friends confide in each other, Jesus shares with us what He has learned from the Father. What an awesome truth!

Jesus befriended Judas, even though He knew that Judas would betray Him.

Perhaps you have known the betrayal of a close friend. You find it hard to trust again. It may cause you to hide from others, never sharing your innermost thoughts or feelings. It is better to trust and experience betrayal than never to have trusted or revealed yourself to anyone.

We cultivate friendship with Jesus by believing His Word, welcoming Him into our lives, experiencing His forgiveness, recognizing His presence daily, talking to Him, confiding our deepest thoughts, dreams, regrets, and sorrows. He is the one friend who will never forsake us. He can go with us even through death. Friendship with Jesus and the practice of opening our hearts to Him can make us secure enough to open ourselves up to others so that we may experience true friendship.

However, friendship with God carries a cost, says Paul J. Wadell, in *Becoming Friends*: "To speak of friendship with God can sound so cozy and consoling, as if we are all snuggling up to God; however, there is no riskier vulnerability than to live in friendship with God, because every friendship changes us, because friends have expectations of each other, and because friends are said to be committed to the same things…Any friend of God is called to faithfully embody the ways of God in the world, even to the point of suffering on account of them. There may be grace and glory in being a friend of God, but there is also clearly a cost."[1]

The Adventure of New Friends

While keeping in touch with old friends, we need to be making new ones.

Friendship is a wonderful way to grow. The times in my life when I grew the most and learned the most were when I pushed myself out of my personal comfort zone and joined new groups or pursued new interests. We are happiest when we are loving and learning, and we do this best with friends. Forming friendships with people who have opinions and interests that differ from mine stretches me, helps me think new thoughts and consider new ideas, as well as providing opportunities to share my faith in Christ.

The Freedom of Friends

What is it you appreciate most about a friend? For me, it is the freedom to be myself, with no pretense. It's not having to weigh my words, to let them pour out, knowing my friend will "blow away the chaff and retain the kernel" of what I'm trying to say. It's knowing that my friend has a tough skin and will forgive me if I unintentionally hurt her. She will be honest with me, even when doing so requires loving correction. She will tell me when my hairstyle isn't flattering, my earrings don't match, or the new outfit I'm considering really does make me look fat!

When my friend disappoints me, I will ascribe to her the best motives possible: I will understand and still think the best. Even when she makes bad choices, I won't forsake her; I will still be her friend, but I will lovingly confront her. I want to be the kind of a friend who is hard to lose—the kind who hangs in there. I believe this is the way to build lifelong friendships

Friendship requires being there when I am needed. It also involves knowing when to back off and allow my friend space to work things out on her own. I respect her privacy and don't pry or barge in when I'm not needed or wanted.

I appreciate friends who challenge me to push beyond my doubts, who encourage me to try new things, who express confidence in my ability to meet life on God's terms.

Praying With a Friend

If you have never prayed aloud with a friend, I challenge you to think about doing this. Find someone you feel close to and present the idea to her. You may find it awkward at first, but push past the discomfort and persevere. Praying together will deepen your friendship. Begin with simple, short prayers, perhaps during a time of sorrow, stress, or testing. Simply say, "Do you think we could pray about this together?"

Masks Hinder Friendship

Don't be afraid to admit your needs to your friend. No one enjoys a whiner, but don't you really prefer someone who can say frankly that she is tired, discouraged, angry, or hurt, rather than someone who maintains a stoic superspirituality?

True friendship must be a two-way street, where one person isn't always the giver or counselor and the other the needy one. The phrase, "Only sinners can relate," expresses the difficulty of relating to someone who never admits any needs or shortcomings, someone who is always ready to help but never needs any help herself.

Not long ago, I read, "If you are spiritual, no one will talk to you."

People who appear perfect are not approachable.

The writer of the Book of Hebrews says that Jesus was tempted in all points just as we are and that He isn't a high priest who can't be touched by the feelings of our infirmities and failures. Because Jesus understands our temptations and trials, He is able to come along side us as a true friend. He doesn't scold us or point to His perfection.

Learning from Job's Friends

You remember Job in the Old Testament who suffered the loss of his treasures, his family, and his health. But he still had his friends! And they came to comfort him. The first man began by sitting quietly with Job, sharing his grief and entering into his sorrow. But later on, all three felt it necessary to deliver long theological treatises, suggesting that Job was suffering because of sins he had committed. Even if that were true, it didn't comfort Job to hear about it. From Job's friends we learn that we don't need to tell people what they already know, that all tragedy isn't the result of sin; we don't know when God is punishing someone, and it's probably better to keep silent if we have no encouraging word to alleviate the suffering of another person.

Things to Think About and Discuss

- Have you ever tried to sound or appear spiritual?
- What effect did it have on those around you?
- When is quoting Scripture to someone a bad idea?
- Friendships take time. Do you ever feel the need to limit the number of your friendships because of this?
- What is the nicest thing a friend ever did for you?

CHAPTER TEN

I'M A MEMBER OF CHRIST'S BODY, THE CHURCH

A little girl attended a circus for the first time. When she returned home she exclaimed, "Oh Mother! If you had ever been to a circus, you would never want to go to church again!"

There are many people who think that the church is boring, unimportant, and irrelevant in today's world, and others wish it could be more like the circus or some other entertaining event. Professed believers are sometimes casual, occasional, and indifferent with regard to church attendance. But Jesus loved the church and gave Himself for her (Ephesians 5:25). It is important to Him that we meet together to worship and edify one another.

Some churches are attempting to change how they *do* church, to make it more relevant and exciting. With a marketing strategy typical of today's world, they aim to give the "consumer" what he or she is looking for. In some larger communities, this has worked to create greater attendance and renewed interest in the message of Christ. But churches in smaller communities feel they can't compete with the professional programming and staff needed to provide such varied and stimulating programs.

What Is the Church?

First of all, we need to define church. What is it?

The church is not essentially something you "go to." Rather, it something you are "a part of." While we often think of a church as a building where we worship, in broad scriptural terms *the church is the universal body of believers*. Jesus is the one who places you in the church, which is *His body on the earth*. This union of all true believers is sometimes referred to as the universal church, in contrast to local churches that meet in buildings across our country and around the world.

According to the Bible, each member of the universal church is part of the others. "So in Christ we who are many form one body, and each member belongs to all the others" (Romans 12:5). The universal church includes true Christians in all parts of the world, regardless of their race, sex, or denominational affiliation.

Jesus doesn't live in church buildings but dwells today in believers through the power of the Holy Spirit. We are His presence in the world. It matters how we represent Him. "Don't you know that you yourselves are God's temple and that God's Spirit lives in you?" said the apostle Paul in 1 Corinthians 3:16. Again, addressing the people at Berea, Paul said, "The God who made the world and everything in it is the Lord of heaven and earth and does not live in temples built by hands" (Acts 17:24).

Your Family and the Church

Since all believers belong to the universal church, some Christians have concluded that belonging to a local church is not important. However, in the Bible, local churches had great importance. Much of the New Testament consists of letters written to young churches of the first century.

Being part of the universal Church does not excuse us from the responsibility to relate to believers on the local level. When the apostle Paul wrote to various churches in the New Testament, he wrote to local churches that actually existed. Believers are to exercise their God-given gifts within the context of a local church. In order to grow effectively as Christians, we need to relate to a local body of believers.

Many families today are not motivated to attend church on a regular basis. This may be due to negative experiences from the past or the fast pace of our culture, with its emphasis on the physical and material, rather than the spiritual side of life. Because of longer work weeks, some two-income families say Sunday is their only day for shopping and family time. The way we use our time reflects our priorities. We do the things that are most important to us.

Will Your Child be Attending Church Ten Years From Now?

Tammy sits beside her parents in the Sunday morning church service. Her father is dozing quietly, her mother imperceptibly preparing a list of items to be purchased at the grocery store on the way home, while the pastor launches into point number three of his half-hour sermon. Tammy stares at the bulletin, reading the prayer list, wondering how Mrs. Beasley, her former Sunday school teacher, now in her 90s, is coming along after her recent surgery. She also wonders about the new family in the middle of the left-hand section of the church, the ones with the tall, attractive teenage son.

Tammy has attended First Church since she was a baby. Next year she will be attending the state university and she looks forward to the freedom to choose whether she will attend church or not, and if she decides to go, what church she will choose. Tammy asked Jesus into her heart when she was five years old and the people in church assured her then that she was on her way to Heaven. She occasionally reads a short portion of the Bible and prays before a test at school or when one of her girlfriends has a problem. But for the most part, her Christian life is a collection of Bible stories and Sunday rituals.

There was a youth group until last year when the youth leader left, but no one has replaced him, and most of the teenagers in the church have found other activities to keep themselves busy.

What will Tammy do when she leaves home to attend the university next year? Will she seek out a church? Will she join a Christian organization on campus? Will Jesus be the one who guides her choices and activities or just a tender memory from her childhood? Does Tammy have a faith that is real enough to meet the challenges of today's world, influence her future choices, and last a lifetime?

The Church and Teens

I remember my teen years, a poignant mix of joy and struggle, wondering who I was and who I would become, desiring to be part of the group, yet wanting to be strong enough to stand apart as an individual.

Following the death of my mother, when I was fifteen years old, Jesus called me to follow Him. I responded, because I thought the God who made me would know best how I should live. It has been a wonderful adventure!

Jesus still calls young people to follow Him. What does that mean in the twenty-first century? Is it simply to go to church? To obey a list of rules—biblical or man-made? How will Tammy look back on her teen years and the decisions she makes as a young adult. How can the church help?

Ecclesiastes 12:1 was written to young people, even though it talks mainly about growing old. It is an admonition to live well. We must not confuse the "good life" with a life well-lived. Living well is not realizing success by man's definition, not achieving wealth or fame but rather living out God's plan for our lives.

Jesus went to the temple when He was twelve years old in the company of His parents, just as all Jewish boys were required to do. Scripture tells us the teachers of the law—the rabbis—were amazed at His wisdom, so much so that Jesus wound up teaching them. Jesus was a serious young man who was already intent on accomplishing His Father's will. But He was Jesus, you say! Ah, yes, but what an example for young people. What is it that makes some teenagers open and receptive to spiritual things and others uncaring and unconcerned?

God's will is "good, pleasing, and acceptable," says the King James Version of Romans 12:2. But sometimes Christians speak of God's plan for their lives as if it were distasteful and undesirable—something to dread. ("Lord, please don't make me go to Africa!") God's plan for our lives is the very best we could choose or experience. Why would anyone want anything else?

Sometimes what is modeled for young people in our churches is empty ritual (show up and go through the motions) and man-made rules, with a few well-chosen Bible verses to assure us we are going to Heaven when we die.

Religion becomes boring after a while, but God never does! A big God, a glorious God, Creator, Savior, Sustainer,

Guide—the one who justifies us and leads us in paths of righteousness—is the God we are called to follow!

Is He the one we are presenting in our churches?

I have talked with believers who said they left the church in their young adult lives and later returned. More frequently than not, during their years of straying, they made choices they regretted, and the consequences of these choices followed them through life.

Why would anyone stop following Christ at such a crucial time in their lives when they could be spared unnecessary mistakes? Can the church prevent this from happening?

Are we presenting the gospel accurately, triumphantly, as the best way to live life? Or do teens see us living pinched lives deprived of joy and longing for the husks of the world?

Our church fusses don't help! When there is division in our churches, we need to ask ourselves if the issues are big enough to cause others to stumble.

Teenagers say:

- Church is boring.
- There are too many rules.
- Christians are crabby.
- The world looks like more fun.
- The church culture is rigid: We cannot (or will not) change.
- One young man said he has long pondered why Christians aren't happier people.
- Another said he wanted to be a Christian because the people he admired most were Christians. A positive comment!

These are questions the church needs to ask:

- What is authentic Christianity?
- Are we genuine in what we do and say?
- Are we presenting the gospel in its entirety?
- Are we teaching and living the abundant life in Christ (John 10:10)?
- Are we creating "false fences"? (Legalism will drive people from Christ.)
- Are we as adult Christians bored with God? Does it show?
- Has our faith become religion?

What Can We Do?

We need to cultivate relationships between generations in our churches. Teenagers need adult friends. Their peers shouldn't be their only influence.

Studies show parents still carry the greatest influence in the lives of their children. Parents must be encouraged not to quit too soon or bail out when their children become teens.

The church can help by being accepting, loving, flexible, and enthusiastic about life in Christ. Our teaching needs to go beyond the plan of salvation and include studies in Christian doctrine and application of Scripture to everyday life. The church should encourage questions and participation by young people.

Taking a Long Look at Church Involvement

Relating to a local body of believers on a week-by-week basis is not always easy. Local churches experience their share of ups and downs, disagreements, financial crises, and doctrinal disputes. However, remaining in a local church, serving according to our spiritual gifts, and fellowshipping with the same family of believers over a period of time can build our spiritual muscles and develop our character. It helps us realize that we are all in process and not yet perfect.

If parents are bored, indifferent, or critical of the church, they will not be able to hide these attitudes from their children. Our attitudes will affect how our children view the church when they are grown and may determine whether they decide to attend. While church attendance in itself doesn't guarantee that our children will follow Christ, it is tremendously important. Studies show it is particularly important that the father attend along with the rest of the family.

However, feeling compelled to be at church each and every time the doors open doesn't always positively influence children. Overinvolvement in church activities can swallow up much needed family time and cause children to feel they are second in importance. Because many pastors and church leaders are aware of this, they try not to schedule activities every night of the week, pulling family members in competing directions.

Serving the church and being involved in too many activities can become a source of ego gratification for parents while negatively influencing the family. Children will not lovingly remember a church that required Mom or Dad to be out every night of the week. Priorities and balance are essential.

Gossip, politicking, and divisions within the church create disturbance in our families. Some say conflict is normal. But I wonder if the issues we quarrel about are big enough to warrant the attention we give them? Before dividing over every wind of doctrine or personal preference, we need to think about the resulting negative impact on our children and the damage to our testimony in the community where we minister.

Churchmanship: What Is It?

A lovingly remembered former pastor used the term, "churchmanship." An old word, a bit archaic perhaps, but I believe it merits dusting off and redefining for believers today.

Churchmanship can be defined as: "The manner in which a person conducts himself within the church body; the ability to worship and serve alongside other believers in a Christ-honoring way."

What topics would be covered in a course on churchmanship? I suggest the following:

- Find your niche. Ask God to direct you to the right church. C. S. Lewis, in the preface to his book, *Mere Christianity*, compares becoming a believer to entering large hall, out of which open doors into many rooms. He instructs us not to remain in the hall too long but to earnestly consider which door is the "true one." Rather than selecting the one that is most appealing, we need to ask, "Are these doctrines true? Is holiness here? Does my conscience move me towards this?"[1] The choice is not to be made on the basis of pride, mere taste, or personal dislike of the doorkeeper. Lewis further cautions us to "Be kind to those who have chosen different doors and to those who are still in the hall."[2]
- Join up. Be a participant, not just an interested bystander. Let them know you're on the team.
- Serve in the area of your spiritual gifts. Don't hide behind false humility. Offer to help—volunteer. If

you can teach, teach. If you have musical ability, let them know. If you can wield a "mean lawn mower," offer to cut the grass.

- Give generously. Consider the largest portion of your tithe as belonging to your local church.
- Be friendly. Seek out the less popular and lonely people, not just those who seem to be movers and shakers. Even if you're new to the group, don't wait for others to greet you. Reach out to them first. Look for people you can encourage.
- Support the leaders of the church. Pray for them. If you have criticisms or suggestions, go directly to the designated leaders rather than sharing your thoughts with other church members.
- Don't listen to gossip. During World War II, there was a phrase: "Loose lips sink ships." They also "sink" churches.
- Go to give yourself, not just to be fed. Your pastor may not be among the top ten in the nation, but give him a chance to minister to you.
- Confront in love. If criticism is in order, be sure you do it in a biblical manner. Matthew 18:15–17 indicates you must first go privately to the offending person before sharing with anyone else.
- Be reliable. Keep the commitments you make. Be on time. Be prepared. If you can't be there, let your church know ahead of time and make arrangements for someone else to fulfill your responsibility. Commitments to ministry in your church deserve the same conscientious consideration you give your secular employer.

Scripture Passages

- Romans 12
- Romans 14:1–15:7
- 1 Corinthians 3:16
- Acts 17:24
- Matthew 18:15–17

Things to Think About or Discuss

- If you were to move to a new town, what would you look for in a church?
- What do you like best about your church?
- Describe what you think would be the ideal church.
- How can we prevent church difficulties or disagreements from having a negative impact on our children?
- How would you answer someone who says the church is full of hypocrites?
- Should the local church change with the times in order to be relevant in today's culture? If yes, in what ways? What, if anything, should never change?
- How have the churches you have attended changed during your lifetime?
- What are some of the things you would include in "a life well-lived?"

CHAPTER ELEVEN

I'M AN ATTRACTIVE PERSON

Remember the wicked stepmother in the story *Snow White*? She worried constantly that there would be someone in her kingdom more beautiful than she. Every day she inquired of her magic mirror: "Mirror, mirror on the wall, who is fairest of them all?" And every day the mirror would reassure her that she was the fairest woman in the land. But one day she received the reply she had dreaded: Snow White, her own stepdaughter, was "fairest of them all."

Most of us will never have the opportunity to be the fairest, whether homecoming queen or winner of a beauty contest. Perhaps it is just as well. When we read the biographies of beautiful people, we often find their lives tragic and complicated. Still, if there were a line forming for those who wished to be beautiful, most of us would join it.

What is beauty? Why do we desire it? In whose eyes is it determined? Is it truly in the eyes of the beholder, or is that only a cliché to make us believe someone, somewhere, could find us beautiful?

"Beauty is as beauty does," we were told as little girls. Still, the prettiest little girls seemed to be adored in ways that the best-behaved were not.

Although some feminists have tried to downplay the importance of a woman's appearance, women's magazines still promote the idea that how a woman looks is most important. Beauty is more highly acclaimed than character.

How does a Christian woman respond to the messages of the world?

How should we instruct our daughters?

Many women are described in the Bible as being beautiful. Nowhere does the Bible disparage beauty. Esther became queen as a result of winning a beauty contest. Sarah, Rebecca, Rachel, and Abigail were all recognized for their beauty. Every woman wants to feel that she is desirable.

We are not told that Eve was beautiful, but Adam found her acceptable. (Of course, she had no competition.) Because she was created before sin entered the world, she was no doubt perfect in every way.

We are not told that Mary, the mother of Jesus, was beautiful, although she may have been. When it came to the supreme honor of becoming the mother of the Messiah and Savior, moral purity was the quality God looked for.

The thirty-first chapter of the Book of Proverbs describes a woman who did it all. Yet verse 30 tells us it was not her beauty or her charm that brought her honor. Rather, her fear of the Lord set her apart. She is portrayed as trustworthy, industrious, compassionate, dignified, and wise.

"She is clothed with strength and dignity; she can laugh at the days to come. She speaks with wisdom and faithful instruction is on her tongue," says Proverbs 31:25–26.

Verse 30 goes on to tell us that "charm is deceptive and beauty is fleeting."

Charm, we all know, is deceptive. The most beautiful woman can be a vixen—shrewd and ill-tempered.

And, although many of us of know women who are attractive in their fifties, sixties, and beyond, the beauty of youth slowly diminishes—hair dye, tummy tucks, and eye jobs, notwithstanding.

Young men are warned in Proverbs 6:20-35 not to lust after the beauty of the immoral woman or the wayward wife. Beauty attracts. This has always been true and remains so today.

While instructing our daughters that beauty is *not* the most important quest in life, perhaps we ought to caution our sons that they could be miserable married to the most beautiful woman in the world.

"Beauty is only skin deep."

"That's deep enough for me!" someone quipped. We laugh at such a remark, but it illustrates the fact that, even when we know that beauty is ultimately unimportant, we still desire it. Decade after decade, we primp and preen pursuing the beauty we believe will make us admired and loved. One of the ways we do this is by playing a game called "fashion."

Playing the Fashion Game

People play many games in life. Fashion is one of them. Whether clothes, home furnishings, or cars, we like to be in style, have the latest, and be "with it," rather than "without it." We do not like to be old fashioned, dowdy, or out-of-style. And so we play into the hands of the marketing strategists. Sales people used to sell us what we needed. Now marketing people "create" needs through television and newspaper advertising, billboards, direct mail, and the Internet. Their messages are designed to make us feel inadequate if we don't have the latest thing. Businesses have dress codes designed to present a certain image. While the game is not wrong in itself, it tends to make us more concerned with the packaging than the person inside. "The medium is the message," said writer Marshall McLuhan.

Several decades ago, character was what gave a person a sense of self worth. People in their communities were recognized as honest, hard-working, reliable, and trustworthy. No one thought much about the brand of clothes they wore. Brand names were hidden, not displayed on the outside of clothing.

Today many people never stay in one community long enough to have any sort of reputation, but rely on the brand of clothes they wear, the model car they drive, or the house they live in, to identify who they are and give them a sense of self-worth.

All of us have a desire to fit in, to be "OK" in the eyes of others. Marketing plays on this desire, enticing us to buy what we can't afford and making us judgmental of those who do not choose to play the fashion game.

Whether we choose to play the fashion game or not, the Bible says we are not to look down upon those who don't. (See James 2:1–4.) We are cautioned not to give preference to people who are dressed in the latest styles while turning away from those who don't look the way we think they should.

Does the Christian Need a Dress Code?

Fashion has long been a hot topic in churches—even in the first century. Women were told in 1 Timothy 2:9 to dress modestly. First Peter 3:3–4 says, "Your beauty should not come from outward adornment, such as braided hair and the wearing of gold jewelry and fine clothes. Instead, it should be that of your inner self, the unfading beauty of a gentle and quiet spirit, which is of great worth in God's sight."

How are we to understand these verses in the light of today's fashions?

The principle of *modesty* continues to be applicable, and a gentle, quiet spirit remains an asset to any woman. Our appearance should bring honor to the one we represent, the Lord Jesus Christ, for we are His ambassadors. As Christians, we represent Him to a lost world (2 Corinthians 5:20).

Christian women should place primary emphasis on their demeanor, character, and personalities. Concern for inward beauty should take precedence over outward adornment. Our character and dispositions are more important than an impressive wardrobe.

A century ago, Christian women were known for their "plainness," lack of makeup, and hair-in-a-bun appearance. But the Bible states we are to "make the teaching about God our Savior attractive" (Titus 2:10). The King James Version uses the word *adorn*. We *can* present an attractive appearance without being fixated on ourselves and our image. The issue is one of *emphasis* and *priority*.

After giving attention to good grooming and appropriate clothing, we can go confidently into the world forgetting ourselves and thinking of others.

Fitness, Fads, and Fanaticism

Imagine what people who died in the first half of the twentieth century would think if they could come back to life today. How would they view joggers running in our streets in shorts and t-shirts? Would they think there was a national emergency and people had no time to grab clothing before fleeing? Suppose they caught sight of the supermarket tabloids advertising ways to improve one's abs? How strange it would seem for ordinary people to worry about particular muscles (and know them by nicknames, such as abs and pects). Would it seem peculiar to them that so many men and women are on diets today, while even greater numbers are overweight? The current emphasis on physical activity would seem odd to those who lived in earlier decades when physical labor provided all the exercise they needed.

Recent studies say maybe butter is better for you than margarine after all. But previous studies indicated margarine was a healthier choice than butter. Of course, soft margarine is better than hard. Some say coffee is bad; others claim to have proven coffee is harmless and may even be good for you. Chocolate will clog your arteries but may make you live longer. Sugar is bad, but artificial sweetener is dangerous too. New studies often contradict the findings of earlier ones. People scrutinize the labels and worry over every bite they consume.

The fact that people, on the average, live longer and better today is partly due to the availability of medications that treat chronic diseases.

When did the fitness craze begin? Was it the 60s? The 70s? Suddenly, it seemed, people were more intent on preserving their bodies than ever before. Aerobics was the new thing back then, or at least most of us hadn't heard about it. Jogging, running, kickboxing, stair-stepping, Yoga, and Tai Chai followed. More people began to exercise. It wasn't just twenty sit ups in your bedroom any more or touching your toes a few times a day. You had to go to special places to "work out." Gyms and fitness centers sprang up all over the country. People purchased exercise bicycles, treadmills, and ski machines by the thousands. You could view video tapes of beautiful scenery while biking, skiing, or running.

These strenuous activities replaced the physical work people used to do. In the last half of the twentieth century fewer people lived on farms and there were no more "chores" to do—no cows to milk or fence posts to sink. Hardly any one walked, since many people lived in suburbs and couldn't easily get to their destinations on foot. Families required two or three cars to get where they were going. And they were going more than ever before. New homes sported two- and three-car garages. Exercise required special clothing made of Spandex, fitting close to the body. Running suits, or wind suits, or sweat suits became the fashion. (You couldn't simply exercise in your old clothes, could you?) You also needed special shoes, ones that cost more than those you wore on Sunday. Or maybe tennies were OK for Sunday too. Today we wear flip-flops!

The Bible says bodily exercise is good. I find going to the local YMCA twice a week a great way to stay fit. First Timothy 4:8 affirms "physical training is of *some* value, but godliness has value for all things, holding promise for both the present life and the life to come."

While it's true that life expectancy has increased, unless the Lord returns in our lifetime, we will all die. Our bodies will wear out and, despite all we can and should do to preserve them, they will not last forever. But godliness counts for eternity. What if, for every hour spent in physical training, Christians spent equal time in the Bible or prayer? Which would profit us more? *Balance* and *priorities* are again necessary.

The Bible describes our bodies as God's temples, sacred because God lives in them (1 Corinthians. 3:16–17). During our lifetimes we have the privilege of serving God in the bodies He has given us. We should preserve and care for them, protecting them from any sort of excess or abuse. God wants to be honored in our bodies.

The Christian's Assurance

Many people in today's culture believe this life is all there is—perhaps that explains the present preoccupation with preserving what is physical, while showing little concern for the spiritual. As Christians we know our bodies are temporary and perishable. But they will be raised imperishable and in power. "Just as we have borne the likeness of the earthly man, so shall we bear the likeness of the man from heaven." That man, of course, is Jesus Christ (1 Corinthians 15:49).

As surely as these bodies wear out, we are promised that we will get new ones. Isn't that good news!

"Dear friends, now we are children of God, and what we will be has not yet been made known. But we know that when he appears, we shall be like him, for we shall see him as he is. Everyone who has this hope in him purifies himself, just as he is pure" (1 John 3:2–3).

Things to Think About or Discuss

- Describe the time in your life when you felt most beautiful.
- Describe a person you have known who was not beautiful in the usual sense but who was beautiful to you.
- How would you console a little girl or a teenager who did not think she was pretty?
- How important is it to you to be in style?
- How can you look up-to-date on a budget?
- How can we apply the standard of modesty in the area of dress today?

- What do you do to exercise or stay fit?
- How do you "exercise" spiritually?

CHAPTER TWELVE

I'M A POSITIVE PERSON

Life Is Attitudinal

Hot tears stung Emily's eyes as she stuffed the remaining papers into her briefcase and slammed the desk drawer shut for the last time. Stillness permeated the empty office as the dwindling light of late afternoon filtered through the dusty blinds.

"Well, good riddance to this job!" she muttered aloud to the gray filing cabinets. "Another job down the tubes! How can I tell Steve? I really thought this one would work out. If only they hadn't expected so much. After all, I'm nobody's slave! Who do they think they are? Overtime? If only other people had carried their share of the load. I'll show them they can't order me around. I don't do overtime, and I certainly can't be expected to pick up the slack if other people don't do what they're supposed to do!"

"Bad attitude," Mr. Garrison had said.

"Well, I've heard that before," she thought.

But the words pierced her heart because she had heard them so often.

"Emily has a bad attitude."

"Emily doesn't get along well with others." (Was that Mrs. Carpenter, her third-grade teacher—or was it Mr. Elliot in sixth?)

"Emily pouts and worries too much about what other people do."

"Emily has an authority problem...."

"Bad attitude..."

Attitudes. What are they? Where do we get them?

Webster's New World College Dictionary defines an attitude as "A manner of acting, feeling, or thinking that shows one's disposition, opinion...."[1]

Attitudes reflect the way we think and feel, usually about things we cannot change. They are the result of collected emotions toward the people and events in our lives. Attitudes indicate our mindset toward life. All of us have attitudes. We catch them from our families; we adopt them as a result of circumstances; we develop them over time.

Our attitudes influence our actions. Negative attitudes can be the result of hurts, disappointments, and wrong thought patterns we learned as children. Some personality types are more likely to be negative than others.

Some of the ways we might express wrong attitudes are:

- Criticism: "He never does anything right!" "I can't stand her!"
- Complaining: "I don't like the way things are." "I don't see why…"
- Arguing: "I am right; you are wrong. I have to prove it."
- Resentment: "It shouldn't have happened to me. How could she do that?"
- Jealousy/covetousness: "Why can't I have what she does?"
- Self-pity: "None of these should have happened. Why did it happen to me?"
- Regret: "Why did things turn out as they did?" "If only…"
- Guilt: "Why did I do (or say) that? I wish I could erase the past."
- Stubbornness: "I won't give in. I can't change. This is the way I am."
- Defensiveness: "It's not my fault." "What do you mean by that?"

Much of our unhappiness results from *our reaction* to what someone else did or did not do. Unfulfilled expectations cause disappointment, resentment, and despair.

Negative attitudes damage us, our families, and our churches.

Examples of Jesus and Paul

Philippians 2:5–11 describes the attitude Jesus Christ had in His earthly life. Though He was God—and equal with God the Father—He did not "count equality with God a thing to be grasped." He knew who He was. He had nothing to prove. He could become a servant because He was secure in God as His heavenly Father. Can knowing who we are in Christ not do the same for us?

The apostle Paul reminds us that God "works in us to will and to work for his good pleasure" (verse 13). Knowing this enabled Paul to serve without complaining or arguing. He expressed a willingness to be "poured out" for the sake of others.

Christians should adopt this same attitude.

First Corinthians 2:16b says, "...we have the mind of Christ."

When Christ comes to live in us, He begins to change us, and He begins with our thoughts and attitudes.

Changing Our Thinking

"It's not what you think you are; it's what you 'think,' you are."

Are your attitudes generally positive or negative? Is your glass half-full or half-empty? Do you consider yourself an optimist or a pessimist? If you are an anxious, worried person, you may be a pessimist. Perhaps you feel you are only being realistic. All Christians should be realists—seekers after truth.

Some recent studies indicate our "happiness" quotient might be set at birth. But such studies are incomplete, and I believe God can move us in a positive direction.

What we think about influences our attitudes.

The apostle Paul, in Philippians 4:2–8, urges us to:

- "Agree in the Lord." Find common ground. Try looking at the situation from another person's point of view. Even if you think they are wrong, it is helpful to understand why they feel as they do. To understand is not to condone.

- "Rejoice in the Lord." Circumstances may change; He does not. He is the eternal constant. Rejoicing in the face of difficulty tells God you trust Him.
- "Be gentle" (moderate, quiet, peaceable) "in quietness and trust is your strength..." (Isaiah 30:15b). "For man's anger does not bring about the righteous life that God desires" (James 1:20).
- Present your requests to God. Leave the matter with Him. He loves you and knows all about you. He understands when others don't.
- Thank God. Claim God's peace, which will guard your heart and your mind. What a promise for emotional strength!
- Think positive thoughts—find what is true, noble, right, pure, lovely, admirable, excellent, and praiseworthy. (There must be something!) It may not change the negative circumstances around you, but you will be a happier and more peaceful person.
- Recognize God's sovereignty: He is God and we are not! He sees the big picture.

Addressing Bad Attitudes

Wrong attitudes skew our judgment, keeping us from seeing straight. They give us wrong perspectives on many issues. The first step in changing negative attitudes is to become aware of them. We can bring our thoughts before the Lord as we pray, confess, and claim 1 John 1:9, which speaks of God's forgiveness. Before Him we can think aloud as we can with a good friend. We can pray concerning the people and circumstances that cause us to feel resentful and honestly talk to God about our feelings.

We can change our perspective. Learn to mentally "walk around" issues to see how they look from other points of view. We must be *willing to change* (it's called repentance) when we see that we are wrong. It is not the true things we believe that hurt us; it is the things we believe *that are not true*. Admit when you are wrong and repent—change your mind. The person who never changes his mind is not someone to be admired.

"The very idea that there is another idea is something gained" (Richard Jeffries, English author, 1848–1887).

Try to view the situation as it is. Don't paint it with a rose-colored brush. Or a black one! Face reality and accept the truth that God "works for the good of those who love him, who have been called according to his purpose." His purpose is to conform you to the likeness of His Son, not just to make you happy (Romans 8:28–29).

Obey the Lord by taking right action whether you feel like it or not.

Watch for what God is doing. Look for His solution to the problem. It will probably not be what you anticipated. Trust Him! You may not understand—trust Him anyway.

Capturing Your Thoughts

Second Corinthians 10:5 tells us to, "take captive every thought to make it obedient to Christ." Many years ago, during a period of great anxiety in my life, I stumbled across this verse in the King James translation of the Bible, which speaks of "casting down imaginations…and bringing into captivity every thought to the obedience of Christ."

I began to ask myself, "Is what I am thinking really true?" Often I found that my imagination had blown the issue out of proportion or that I had *assumed* things I didn't know for sure. It was during that time that I began to learn the mental discipline of replacing my anxious thoughts with dependence on the promises of God. This is a daily, moment-by-moment discipline, which I am still learning.

When bad attitudes fill our minds and emotions, we need to ask, "Am I overreacting?" "How does this look from someone else's point of view?" "Will it make any difference a year from now?" "Is there an area of obedience I have overlooked?" "Is there someone whose forgiveness I need to seek?"

Ask Christ to change your attitude and help you see things from His perspective. Commit the situation to Him and think about something else. Find a friend to spend time with; choose a Bible verse to think about; go help someone; read a good book; all of these actions will help shake the thoughts that trouble you. Ask God to fill your mind with what pleases Him.

Radio, television, newspapers, books, and magazines bombard us daily with philosophies that are contrary to biblical thinking. While we need to be informed and aware of what is happening in our culture, we must not be unduly influenced or "squeezed into the mold" of the world around us. When we absorb what we hear and read without questioning it, we become conditioned to accept error as truth.

Studying the Bible enables us to resist unbiblical thinking. Christian radio, books, magazines, and tapes are great aids to getting God's Word into our minds and shaping right attitudes. Gaining a biblical perspective enables us to examine the values and ideas presented by the media and helps us to develop a Christian worldview.

Scripture Passages to Consider

- Philippians 2:5–18
- Philippians 4:2–8

- 2 Corinthians 10:5
- 1 John 1:9
- Colossians 3:15–17

Things to Think About or Discuss

- Describe a time when you had a change of attitude toward a person or circumstance.
- What can we do to pass along good attitudes to our children?
- What differences do you see in women's attitudes today compared with generations of women in the past?
- How have your attitudes been influenced by today's culture?
- Why is it hard to let go of bad attitudes?

CHAPTER THIRTEEN

I'M A HAPPY PERSON

The speaker was middle-aged, perky, and blond. She spoke at a conference I attended many years ago, and I don't even remember her name.

But I haven't forgotten her question: "Are you fun to live with?"

She was speaking to Christians, and her question made me think. Up to that time I assumed Christians were serious people—serious about everything—super-analytical, somber, and even a bit sanctimonious. Perhaps they could be called a "blessing," or an "inspiration," or they were "sweet," but "*fun to live with*"? Well, hardly. Christians were people with no anger, no fears, and no feelings (at least none that were acknowledged). They never shouted or giggled!

Today the pendulum seems to have gone in the opposite direction; Christians are encouraged to always be upbeat, to "praise the Lord anyway" with little thought of confronting difficult situations or solving personal problems. Constantly and incessantly, we are to rejoice. Such a person may be just as hard to live with as the soulful sister previously described.

What do we do with our feelings as Christians? How do we handle anger, bitterness, envy, fear, and depression? Do we acknowledge them or deny them? Unbelievers and sometimes our children see through our denial and may conclude that we have made up "sweet stories" to cushion the blows of reality in our lives. No one knows us better than the people with whom we live, except for God.

Honesty, humility, and hope can make us more pleasant to be around and remove some of the emotional barriers that prevent us from being fun to live with.

Honesty Before God

Emotionally honest people are fun to live with.

Because we are prone to hide from ourselves and others, we often think we can hide from God too. When down times strike in our lives, we need to be honest in our prayers. Rather than making up pretty homilies, we can "tell it like it is" when we talk to God. He created us and knows us.

David said in Psalm 139:1–4: "O Lord, you have searched me and you know me. You know when I sit and when I rise; you perceive my thoughts from afar. You discern my going out and my lying down; you are familiar with all my ways. Before a word is on my tongue you know it completely, O Lord."

The Bible has much to say about truth. Psalm 51:6 tells us: "Surely you desire truth in the inner parts; you teach me wisdom in the inmost place."

Proverbs 23:23 commands us to "Buy the truth and do not sell it; get wisdom, discipline and understanding."

Because we are fallen people, it's difficult for us to discern the truth about ourselves and the situations in our lives. But we are commanded to seek truth and not deceive ourselves. Before God we can freely acknowledge our emotions. The Bible declares that truth is freeing (John 8:32).

When we describe a person as not being real, we are sensing that this person is not emotionally honest. The characters in the Bible were real people; they are described as they were, their commendable qualities and their sins recorded for us.

Humility Helps

Humble people are easy to live with. Not those who are *trying* to be humble but those who know they are accepted by God and can forget themselves, at least some of the time. Someone said, "God is not offended by our humanity, but by our posturing and pretense."

God's grace assures us we are accepted by Him because of Jesus' death and resurrection. Therefore, we have nothing to prove. People who need to prove they are OK, or better yet, superior to others, are difficult to be around. They can never relax and just be themselves to the glory of God. And they often compare themselves to others. Second Corinthians 10:12 says, "We do not dare to classify or compare ourselves with some who commend themselves. When they measure themselves by themselves and compare themselves with themselves, they are not wise."

"When pride comes, then comes disgrace, but with the humility comes wisdom," says Proverbs 11:2. A humble person is teachable. She doesn't think she already knows it all but is open to learning new ways. For this reason, Proverbs 15:33 says that "humility comes before honor." According to 1 Peter 5:6–10, humility leads to peace, self-control, and the ability to go through suffering while growing firm and steadfast.

Hope In God

Hopeful people are fun to live with.

The psalmist in Psalm 42:5–6 asks himself, "Why are you downcast, O my soul? (the King James Version reads "disquieted") Why so disturbed within me? Put your hope in God; for I will yet praise him, my Savior and my God."

After seeking the true cause of his distress, David affirms that he will praise God again. He looks ahead and sees a better future. He also wills to remember God in his pain. What we often need most in our down times is a sense of perspective—remembering what God has done in the past and what He will yet do in the future.

I heard about a woman who said her favorite Bible verse was "And it came to pass." While I wouldn't say it is my favorite verse, I have learned that all things do come to pass. And God is still there with our best interest in mind.

When Elijah experienced fear and depression following his flight from the wicked Jezebel (1 Kings 19), God sent an angel who commanded him to eat and then allowed him to rest and sleep. After Elijah was refreshed and renewed, God spoke with him on Mount Horeb. Elijah had the idea he was the only one faithful to the true God, but the Lord assured him there were seven thousand others in Israel who had not bowed to Baal. Depression damages our perspective. The Lord met Elijah's most basic needs for food and rest before attempting to correct his perception. In a similar way, we need to care for our physical health, getting proper rest and a balanced diet.

Throughout the Psalms we are encouraged to *hope* in God and to *wait*. The word *expect* can be substituted in many instances. We can be assured God knows the difficulties we face. He will be with us in our trials and deliver us in His time. Hope believes that God has a plan and something better is ahead. Hebrews 11:1 says, "...faith is being sure of what we hope for and certain of what we do not see." We hope in God's Word. The promises of God have long been a comfort to Christians in times of difficulty. In our sad moments it is better to hang on to what we *know*—the promises of God—than to look to our emotions. While feelings enhance and enrich life, they are not a reliable basis for decision making.

Women and Their Emotions

Women are thought to be more emotional than men. Maybe it's only the way in which we express our emotions. Our society seems to overlook a man's display of anger but labels tears as "womanly." Men are more often taught to hide or deny their emotions. The Bible indicates we are to take responsibility for our emotions, not deny them but control them. We are commanded not to sin in our anger (Ephesians 4:26). We are allowed to grieve but not as those who have no hope (1 Thessalonians 4:13).

I read about a man who murdered his stepdaughter in a fit of rage and later sued the counseling center for not helping him to control his anger. Like many people, he expected to escape personal responsibility for his uncontrolled emotions. But God intends us to bear the fruit of the Holy Spirit described in Galatians 5:22, 23, which includes self-control.

Many women experience a monthly emotional swing that is tied to hormonal changes. Our families may dread this time of month, finding us hard to live with as our emotions surge out of control. Women in menopause may experience similar emotional changes. Again, honesty and humility can be helpful. We need to pray to remain on an even emotional keel during these times so our families don't suffer.

While prayer and reliance on God's promises may be our primary defenses, a willingness to get help from our family doctor or counselor is evidence of humility. It is not unspiritual or unscriptural to take medication when prescribed by a doctor or to seek counseling. Our problems don't excuse lack of consideration for the people in our homes.

Things to Think About or Discuss

- Do you think women are more moody than men? Discuss.
- How do you cope with "the blues"?
- How have others helped you to overcome emotional struggles or depression?
- What Bible verses have comforted you in times of trouble?
- Is depression a spiritual problem or a medical one?
- Do you think Jesus was ever depressed? If so, give an example.
- What is the difference between self-control and denying our emotions?

CHAPTER FOURTEEN

I'M A BALANCED PERSON

John the Baptist wouldn't be considered a balanced person in today's culture. He dressed in camel's hair, existed on a curious diet of locusts and wild honey, and made his home in the wilderness. Even in the day in which he lived, he was probably considered eccentric. Yet, multitudes sought him out, including the Pharisees and Sadducees, the religious leaders of that day. Jesus said, "Among those born of women there has not risen anyone greater than John the Baptist." Then He added, "Yet he who is least in the kingdom of heaven is greater than he" (Matthew 11:11).

Similarly, those who strive to think and live biblically in today's culture will not be considered balanced by everyone.

Webster's New Collegiate Dictionary defines balance as "mental or emotional steadiness, poise, stability."[1] To be balanced is to be moderate, temperate, not violent, intense or severe, keeping within reasonable limits, having boundaries, not going to harmful extremes.

When sin entered the world, one of the qualities mankind lost was balance. When we place our faith in Jesus Christ and His sacrifice for our redemption, God begins to restore the lost balance in our lives. It does not happen overnight and only as we learn to "live for an audience of One," as the Puritans did. We must become God-pleasers rather than man-pleasers.

The Bible defines this quality as wholeness, soundness, or maturity. The word rendered *perfect* in many English translations refers to a believer's maturity or full growth. Madeleine L'Engle, addressing Christians in the arts, writes in her book, *Walking on Water, Reflections on Faith and Art*: "If to be in a healthy state of mind means to be whole (not divided into left and right), and if to be whole means to be holy, then wholeness is what the Christian artist seeks. It is what the Christian seeks."[2]

One of the marks of balance or wholeness is single-mindedness, serving one master. James 1: 8 describes "a double-minded man" as being "unstable in all he does."

The word *eccentric* refers to being off center. Our lives will be out of balance until they are centered in Christ. He must be the one we try to please above all others (Colossians 1:10).

We must purposefully seek to live biblically.

The marquee of one church reads: "The main thing is to keep the main thing the main thing," a good description of a biblically balanced life.

The Bible gives many examples of balance: We are given the gift of work yet encouraged to set aside one day in seven for rest. We can be angry but not sin; sorrow but not as those who have no hope; be saved by grace, but our faith is to be evidenced by our works. Husbands must love their wives, but wives must respect their husbands; children should obey their parents, but parents shouldn't exasperate their children.

From the library of an old church I purchased a book by E. S. Jones: *Is the Kingdom of God Realism?* published in 1940. In his book he describes an acquaintance in this manner: "Until the moment of his self-surrender he was like a flywheel in a great factory which had slipped off the center and was shaking itself and the building to pieces, a thing of destruction to itself and its surroundings. But the moment he slipped into the will of God he was like the flywheel back on its center, now going around with rhythm, power, and constructive energy. He had found his center—the will of God."[3]

Biblical balance will enable us to do the right thing, for the right reason, to the right degree. It will enable us to choose wisely from the many opportunities for service. "Wisdom," someone has said, "consists in knowing what to leave out." Wisdom also knows when to quit and how much is too much.

Such discernment enables us to respond when others need our help and know when our assistance enables them to continue making poor choices.

A biblical perspective will influence our reactions, as well as our actions, enabling us to hold firm convictions, while acknowledging there are opinions other than our own. Objectivity, rooted in biblical understanding, will enable us to see the bad in the good and the good in the bad in situations, movements, and ideas. (See Colossians 2:8 and Hebrews 5:14.)

What Balance Is Not

Balance is not blandness or mediocrity. It is not being somewhat honest, relatively moral, slightly caring, moderate in conviction, and generally wishy-washy. It is not being "medium" or middle-of-the-road on everything. A balanced Christian can seek excellence, be strong in conviction, and serve God with a whole heart. We may be called, as John the Baptist was, to do or say things that are contrary to the pervading culture. Many fervent Christian leaders of the past would be called unbalanced by today's standards.

But the balanced Christian also has a sense of proportion and perspective, knows when to speak and when to be silent, and understands which issues are big enough to stand up for. Balance is seeing the big picture and taking the long look. We do not need to react emotionally to everything that happens, but we can allow God time to calm us down and clear our thinking.

In Matthew 6:33, Jesus taught us to seek what is lasting and eternal. This will help us not to "sweat the small stuff."

A friend of mine said her parents held the philosophy, "if a little is good, a lot is better," which led them to overdo church attendance.

Consider your favorite cake recipe. You would not add equal amounts of salt and flour. Varying amounts of each ingredient are needed. It's a matter of knowing how much. And too much is too much. Careful measurements insure a successful result.

How often we are inclined to "add on a little" when quoting Scripture, take a verse out of context, string a few verses of Scripture together to prove a point, or twist the meaning to fit our convictions. We may push our positions so far they cease to be biblical. In this way we turn people off to the gospel and alienate Christian brothers and sisters who don't see things our way.

Harmful Extremes

Most of us are familiar with caricatures, either from newspapers, magazines, circuses, or fairgrounds. When drawing a caricature, the artist takes an identifying feature and exaggerates it. Though the person or object drawn is instantly recognizable, the picture doesn't represent a true likeness. In the same way, Christians can blow an area of doctrine or a particular conviction out of proportion. This form of imbalance tends to cause others to turn away from the truth we are trying to convey.

Unbalanced Christians often become stumbling blocks to others. Romans 14:16 tells us: "Do not allow what you consider good to be spoken of as evil." Compulsive rituals, legalistic compliance with traditions, and being overly-conscientious can appear as religiosity or self-righteous "niceness." Our families are quick to pick up on this. "All our righteous acts are like filthy rags," says the Scripture (Isaiah 64:6). Self-righteousness is always ugly.

We all know people who overcompensate for a lack of balance in the homes in which they grew up. The person who grew up in a home that was fastidiously clean may be purposefully sloppy. Another reacting to a parent's extreme frugality may become a spendthrift. Or consider the individual with workaholic parents who overcompensates by being lazy and uninvolved.

It isn't necessary to go to one extreme to avoid the other.

We can miss out on joy and adventure in life by being overcautious, as a result of witnessing harmful extremes in the lives of our parents or other people.

Perhaps we have watched someone share their Christian faith in a pushy manner that we don't want to emulate and this has quenched our desire to participate in any form of evangelism.

"Extremes produce moderates," I have heard.

Sometimes extremes produce opposite extremes.

Maintaining Balance

Being a God-pleaser rather than a man-pleaser is a safeguard against losing our balance. We should choose areas of service that are in line with the spiritual gifts God has given us. Not everyone needs to do everything. While Christians can be good examples and "spur one another to good works," we need to follow Christ and not the crowd. Christians are sometimes more *driven* to meet the expectations of others than they are *led* into areas where God wants them to serve.

Knowledge and understanding of the Scripture will help us retain the big picture and the small stuff will not seem so important. We are told in Ephesians 4:14–15: "Then we will no longer be infants, tossed back and forth by the waves, and blown here and there by every wind of teaching," but instead, "speaking the truth in love, we will in all things grow up into him who is the Head, that is Christ."

Following this instruction will prevent us from following fads of doctrine that may be emphasized from time to time or from being drawn into every difference of opinion. God wants to give us wisdom and perspective as He matures us spiritually and emotionally.

Christian brothers and sisters can help us. Their input into our lives is important. But only Jesus is perfectly balanced. We need biblical teaching in a church that has a balanced ministry. Fellowshipping with and working alongside believers of other persuasions can keep us from becoming dogmatic and thinking our view is the only one.

Studying Christian history will prevent us from resisting changes in church traditions. Learning that altar calls originated during the Second Great Awakening and not with the apostles prevents us from thinking every church service must end in one. Recognizing that hymns sung hundreds of years ago were once thought too modern to be sung in churches will give us perspective on disputes about modern church music.

The Addiction that Brings Praise

If you are a workaholic or a "volunteeraholic," people will praise you. Although these addictions will bring positive recognition, they are not what God desires for us. The term "'work addict' is a broad term that covers rushaholics, careaholics and busyaholics—any person who is driven to do too much,"[4] writes Diane Fassel, author of *Working Ourselves to Death: The High Cost of Workaholism and the Rewards of Recovery*. It can indicate deeper problems, such as depression or low self-esteem. Unfortunately, Christians and churches sometimes promote such a lifestyle, arguing that because our cause is unquestionably worthy, it justifies any sacrifice. We need to examine our motives for maintaining a driven lifestyle or continually busying ourselves with the lives of other people in an attempt to help them.

Attaining balance in our lives may require that we cut out some activities, say no to the good in order to pursue the best, or discontinue an area of previous service so that we can follow God in a new direction. Ecclesiastes 3:1–8 notes there is a time for everything. But everything does not need to be done at the same time!

Scripture Passages to Consider

- Matthew 3:1–10
- Ecclesiastes 3:1–8
- Hebrews 5:11–14
- Isaiah 64:6
- Ephesians 4:14–16
- Colossians 1:9–14
- Colossians 2:6–8
- James 1:2–8

Things to Think About or Discuss

- Describe an area of your life where you have difficulty maintaining balance. What could you do about it?
- In what way could your lack of balance in this area affect your family or others close to you?
- Why might an obedient Christian appear unbalanced in our present culture?

CHAPTER FIFTEEN

I'M A COMMUNICATOR

The Encounter

The ability to communicate through speech is a special gift given to man by God.

Thomas Mann, German author (1875–1955), said, "Speech is civilization itself. The word, even the most contradictory word, preserves contact—it is silence which isolates."

When was the last time you talked with someone who made you feel "heard?" When did you last listen to someone without inwardly waiting for them to finish so you could either end the conversation or make a point of your own? Most of us feel isolated and lonely when we do not have meaningful contact with others.

Swiss psychiatrist, Paul Tournier, who became the intimate confidante of men and women of all ages, called this "encounter." In his book, *The Listening Ear*, he states that people came to him "determined for once in their lives to speak the truth about themselves, instead of constantly having to weigh up what they should or should not be saying."[1]

Most of us are hungry for this sort of encounter—for understanding, for someone to whom we can reveal our innermost selves. Some people have the gift of coming alongside, of accompanying us on life's journey. They are capable of not just sympathy but empathy.

If there have been such people in your life, you are blessed. What must a person bring to create such an encounter? I believe it is acceptance. We must give people the freedom to be who they are. It is sympathy with all sorts of conditions and tolerance of human diversity. All people are sinners.

Honesty, caring, and humor are also involved. People who laugh together, who share a common sense of humor, experience closeness. Such persons are easy to be with, make no demands, are not easily offended, and are quite non-judgmental. Those with imagination are especially delightful because they have the ability to see life from points of view other than their own. I have always wanted to be that sort of person, haven't you?

Dr. Tournier says, "It is rare for people to open their hearts to each other in this way, even in the case of married couples, or close friends. When I question the person who has just told me something he has never dared to admit to anyone else, he replies, 'I was afraid of not being understood.' That is it: he has felt he was understood. The feeling that he is understood is what helps him to live, to face any problem, however difficult, without being false to himself."[2]

"Human beings constantly seek each other and at the same time flee from each other…True dialog is very rare—in conversations each follows his or her own line; ideas pass each other by without meeting…Men and women are lonely in their search for the heart of the matter, for personal contact.[3]

"So what is it that helps people? Certainly not advice, for they either accept it blindly, or they reject it. In either case it does no good. What helps people is...an encounter with people who talk honestly about their own distress, their difficulties, their frustrations, their rejections, and their evasions."[4]

Many Christians can't do this because they have been taught that all complaining is wrong. They think should just "bear up" and never share their needs with others. This is stoicism, not biblical teaching.

In his chapter on "The Power of Listening and the Power of Silence," Dr. Tournier notes, "Modern people lack silence. They no longer lead their own lives; they are dragged along by events. It is a race against the clock. I think what so many people come to see me for is to find a quiet, peaceful person who knows how to listen and who isn't thinking all the time about what he has to do next. If your life is chock-full already, there won't be room for anything else. Even God can't get anything else in. So it becomes essential to cut something out."[5]

The Importance of Words

The most common way we seek to encounter others is through conversation, "an open exchange of intimate feelings" (*Webster's New World College Dictionary*).[6]

Conversation that includes genuine encounter is one of the casualties of our busy lives and our pursuit of material things. Listen to the conversations around you and note how much of our talk relates to our houses, clothes, cars, and other possessions.

I like to compare conversation to a game of catch. In deference to good sportsmanship, one should not hold the ball too long or return it in a direction far from the playing field. A good game requires paying attention.

Comments such as "Nice day!" or "Wasn't that a terrific ball game!" are pleasant greetings but seldom lead to meaningful dialog and leave us hungry for something more.

Meaningful dialog is built on trust and the ability to "come alongside." It is the capacity to identify with another. This is what Jesus did when He came to our world. He came to be one of us, beginning as a tiny baby, to experience life from our point of view, to live the perfect life, go to the cross to pay the penalty for our sin, and rise again, demonstrating His victory and eternal provision for us. He lives, and because He lives, we too can live—now—abundantly and eternally in His presence.

Words matter to God, so much so that He identifies Himself as "the Word," in John 1:1: "In the beginning was the Word, and the Word was with God, and the Word was God. He was with God in the beginning." Our God is a God who communicates with us through Jesus, the living Word, and through the Bible, His written word. Our God is not silent but reveals Himself to us in the person of Jesus Christ.

Just as God's Word reveals who He is, our words reveal who we are.

In Matthew 12:34b, Jesus said, "For out of the overflow of the heart the mouth speaks."

Some words are hard to speak—words such as "I was wrong," "I'm sorry," "I forgive you," or even, "I love you." These words reveal our deepest feelings and struggles. We fear revealing ourselves to others lest we be found unacceptable and rejected.

Families may have difficulty communicating for a number of reasons. Our exchanges are often emotional; we prejudge, interrupt, get our feelings hurt, become angry, offended, and back off. Then we retreat to safe subjects, such as sports, the weather, or events of the day. Sometimes we stop listening altogether, close off, and live in emotional isolation. Confrontation requires an emotional maturity we don't possess.

So we remain hidden from one another, feeling cold and alone but unwilling to risk coming out of our hiding places.

Sins of the Tongue

The Bible speaks a lot about our words and speech. But fear of offending must not lead us to not speak at all or to hide our true feelings from one another.

Titus 2:8 instructs us to "show integrity, seriousness and soundness of speech...."

Proverbs 25:11 says, "A word aptly spoken is like apples of gold in settings of silver."

Jesus said, "But I tell you that men will have to give account on the Day of Judgment for every careless word they have spoken. For by your words you will be acquitted, and by your words you will be condemned" (Matthew 12:36–37).

Having to give account of our words is a sobering thought.

Two of the Ten Commandments given in Exodus 20 concern speech, warning against the misuse of God's name and bearing false testimony against others. We can become so accustomed to hearing the name of God used carelessly that we slide into such phrases as "Oh, my God!" or "Oh, God!"—expressions heard frequently today, which would not have been thought acceptable in the past and remain an affront to God.

Colossians 3:8–10 says, "But now you must rid yourselves of all such things as these: anger, rage, malice, slander, and filthy language from your lips Do not lie to each other, since you have taken off your old self with its practices and have put on the new self, which is being renewed in knowledge in the image of its Creator."

Because filthy talk is so much a part of literature and entertainment today, many people—sometimes even Christians—have lowered their standards. But God has not lowered His and we are all accountable to Him.

Proverbs 10:19 says, "When words are many, sin is not absent, but he who holds his tongue is wise."

Sometimes, following a time of extended conversation with friends, I have thought back over the things I said and asked myself, "Were my words pleasing to God? Did I slander anyone?"

In his epistle, James tells us it is difficult to tame the tongue. Those who can do it, he says, are perfect. (And there is no one who meets that standard.) He goes on to describe the destruction that can be caused by idle and malicious speech. (See James 3:2–6.)

In chapter 4 he deals with slander and judging one's neighbor. (See James 4:11–12.) In our families and in our churches we have seen the damage that can be done by slander and judging others.

"And whatever you do, whether in word or deed, do it all in the name of the Lord Jesus, giving thanks to God the Father through Him" (Colossians 3:17).

This should be our goal as believers.

Scripture Passages to Consider

- Psalm 12:2
- Psalm 36:3
- Psalm 55:21
- Psalm 59:12
- Proverbs 10:19–21
- Proverbs 18:4
- Proverbs 26:22, 28
- Ecclesiastes 5:3
- Ecclesiastes 10:14a
- Ecclesiastes 12:11
- John 1:1–14
- Romans 16:18

Things to Think About or Discuss

- Recall a time when someone said something that encouraged you.
- Recall a time when you said something that encouraged someone else.
- Was the family in which you grew up a "talking" family? What subjects did you discuss? What subjects were not discussed?
- If you grew up in a home where there was little real communication, how did this affect your later relationships?
- Do you think it is possible to communicate honestly without being unloving?
- How can fear of saying the wrong thing cause us to hide from others?
- What are some difficult things you feel you should talk about with your children?
- At what ages is this most difficult? Suggest ways to help open doors to communication.

- What are some ways people avoid meaningful communication?
- What is the difference between flattery and a compliment?

CHAPTER SIXTEEN

I Can Share My Faith

The disciples climbed the mountainside near Bethany—only eleven of them now with Judas gone.

But Jesus was with them. And He was alive! The risen Christ! They had seen Him die, and now He was with them. Numerous times He had appeared to them. They had seen Him, touched Him, and watched Him eat with them.

Matthew 28:16–20 says they worshipped Him there. Perhaps they bowed down, prostrated themselves on the ground, held His hands, talked, laughed, and hugged Him.

In parting, He gave them a command: He said, "All authority in heaven and earth has been given to me. Therefore go and make disciples of all nations, baptizing them in the name of the Father and of the Son and of the Holy Spirit, and teaching them to obey everything I have commanded you. And surely I am with you always, to the very end of the age" (Matthew 28:18–20).

Maybe He said more. We don't know.

I have so many questions. What kind of day it was? Was it warm? Was there grass on the mountainside? Or simply rocks. Did they bring a picnic lunch? Did they know He was preparing to leave them?

What did they do next?

"Then they worshiped him and returned to Jerusalem with great joy. And they stayed continually at the temple, praising God" (Luke 24:52–53).

Are we—believers today—still a part of the Great Commission to go and make disciples?

All of us?

Or was the charge given that day only for the disciples of Jesus' day plus a few called-out ones in each age? Do all believers today have the responsibility of carrying the good news to someone, somewhere? I believe they do.

We usually attach great significance to the last words people speak. And Jesus' words have motivated thousands, perhaps millions, to go into all parts of the world to share the gospel.

Jesus had told them earlier about the harvest. In Luke 10:2, He said, "The harvest is plentiful, but the workers are few. Ask the Lord of the harvest, therefore, to send out workers into his harvest field."

Am I one of those He wants to send? Are you?

A missionary with a Christian organization designed to reach homemakers told me that she doesn't find Christian women today as anxious to share the gospel as they were ten or twenty years ago. What are the reasons for this?

Is it because we no longer consider it politically correct to share our faith?

Sharing the gospel has always carried risks, and few of us are risk-takers. We feel we will lose the approval of others, be seen as interfering in their personal lives, and incur personal rejection.

Many people are no longer certain what the gospel (or good news) really is. "Besides," some say, "Don't we need to respect the fact that everyone has their own idea about God?"

What Is the Gospel?

So what is the gospel, or good news? Has it changed? In 1 Corinthians 15:3–4, the apostle Paul says, "I passed on to you as of first importance that Christ died for our sins according to the Scriptures, that he was buried, that he was raised on the third day according to the Scriptures."

The message does not change. The methods of presenting it can, should, and do.

Living In the World We Live In

None of us can live in the world of the past. We cannot live in the world of tomorrow. We can only live today. And the world has changed. This generation's view of themselves, society, government, institutions, and God is different from the views widely held thirty or forty years ago. Many changes occurred in the turbulence of the sixties, and our culture has not been the same since. These changes affect how people respond to the gospel.

Our mission field has come where we are. The United States is viewed by The Navigators, a well-known mission organization, as the fifth largest mission field in the world. We are no longer viewed as a Christian nation. Christian truth has faded in the last two generations and many people no longer believe in "absolutes" (things that are true for all people, in all places, at all times). Nor do they have any fixed ideas of right and wrong. When we share Christian truth with such persons, they have no idea what we are talking about. They do not understand our "Christianese," (terms understood only by other Christians, especially those of our own denomination or group) and they view our message as irrelevant.

Logical thinking, based on known truth, is often held up to ridicule today. In its place is "mosaic thinking," a little of this and a little of that. The opinion of a movie star or talk-show host, a bit of Eastern philosophy, a smattering of Christian teaching, all pieced together, reminiscent of a mosaic floor.

The United States is viewed as a pluralistic society. There are many religions in our country. To regard any of them as absolute truth is considered intolerant today. And intolerance seems to be the only sin left. People are tolerant of everything except those they view as intolerant.

Many people believe all truth is relative. They say, "It may be true for you, but not for me."

If you declare that anything is wrong for everyone—things such as lying, cheating, swearing, adultery, sex outside of marriage, etc.—you are said to be inflicting your values on others and judging them by your standards. You will be called intolerant!

There is an absence of acknowledged guilt because people have no knowledge of God's standards. They have been taught that guilt is outmoded and damaging to their self esteem. Dr. Laura Schlesinger's book, *The Ten Commandments*,[1] was published in 1998. Dr. Schlesinger is Jewish. I believe she has done all of us a service in bringing to public attention the laws of God.

God's law is the mirror in which we see ourselves guilty before a holy God. Grace is meaningless to those who do not see themselves condemned and in need of pardon.

In place of guilt, many people feel shame. Deep inside they know something is wrong. Since they do not feel guilty for what they have done (because in today's world nothing is intrinsically wrong), they often feel shame for who they are, for the emptiness and lack of meaning in their lives.

Relational Evangelism

Our mission field has arrived—it is all around us. How does Jesus expect us to respond to the changed world in which we live?

First of all, unless we are specifically called to another place, we can be glad we don't have to travel, raise support, or learn a new language to get to our "mission field."

Then again, maybe we do need to learn a new language in order to communicate with our present culture. Certainly we need to be other-person centered, not simply repeating Christian clichés that others do not understand.

Many missionaries, on arrival at their particular place of service, spend much time simply being with the people to whom they are called. But Christians in America sometimes shun unbelievers as friends. Because we object to elements of their lifestyle, we distance ourselves from them, preferring to spend our time with other believers. Would you support a missionary who spent all his time with the other missionaries and never related to the people to whom he was sent?

What Does It Mean to "Pre-Evangelize"?

A number of years ago, I was assigned to write an article regarding Vince DePaoli, a church planter in Rochester,

New York.[2] He was then pastoring a church that met on Sunday mornings in the barroom of a local hotel. Many of the people who attended had given up on church. In my interview with him, Pastor Vince defined his ministry as "pre-evangelism"—bringing people from one growth step to another. On Easter Sunday, 1998, thirty-one new families visited his church. Many of these people were not yet believers but seekers. They needed to be taught what it would mean to believe in Jesus Christ and why they needed Him.

When seekers are asked to make decisions for Christ, they must know what it is they are deciding, what following Christ requires, and the reasons for making such a commitment. I believe we need to always be examining our methods of evangelism.

Examining Our Methods of Evangelism

Is a bad method better than none at all? Sometimes it is. God is sovereign and all of us have heard of people who were converted on street corners by someone who simply told them they were going to hell if they did not repent.

But, why not use methods that are appropriate to our listeners? Jesus tailored His message to His hearers. Paul the apostle also considered his audience and spoke accordingly. Our message does not change, but it sometimes must be "sent to a new location" because the world has moved on.

All of us can have a part in the harvest, the adventure of influencing others toward a vital faith in a living Savior. We are not all called to do this in the same way.

Consider the following suggestions:

- We need to depend on the Holy Spirit to draw people to Christ. How can we know if He is at work in someone? By listening, being sensitive, and trying to understand what God is already doing. How does this person think? How does he see himself? How does he understand God?

- Be a friend. Don't "aim to convert." Only God can bring your friend to an understanding of what it means to believe in Christ. Be available to discuss spiritual topics, but don't turn every conversation into a gospel presentation. Be natural and not overbearing.
- Give honest answers to honest questions. Don't be afraid to say you don't know. Perhaps you can find out. Share biblical truth when you have the opportunity, but don't preach. Allow the Holy Spirit to work through the Word of God.
- Allow time for the Holy Spirit to work in the heart of your friend. It takes nine months to grow a physical baby; it could take even longer for the Holy Spirit to reveal the truth that causes your friend to be born into God's family.
- Remember you may be one link in a chain of people God is using. Allow other believers to get to know your friend. Invite her to places where she can meet other believers.
- Keep confidences that are shared. No one wants to be a "project" or a "target." Although you may want other believers to be praying for your friend, respect her privacy and do not share her specific needs with others, even under the guise of a "prayer request."
- You may want to ask your friend if she is ready to follow Christ in personal faith. Be prepared to share Scriptures that will help her see why she needs Christ and what it means to receive Him into her life.

- After your friend has come to personal faith in Christ, encourage her to share the news with others.
- Continue to stand by and encourage. God often grows His saints through trials and difficulties. The first days, weeks, and months after conversion are usually difficult. Help your friend learn to study the Bible and apply it to life's situations. Remember that God changes us through the renewing of our minds.

The steps of evangelism listed above are not spectacular or difficult. They will not lead to quick decisions or repeat-after-me prayers. Patience and trust are required to wait for God to work. But our friendships with unbelievers can result in their becoming Christians who understand the decisions they have made and who follow Christ with their lives. We cannot always know the result of our influence in the lives of others. But God knows, and He wants us to be part of the grand adventure of spreading the good news!

Things to Think About or Discuss

- Are the words *witness* and *disciple* verbs or nouns?
- What do you fear most about sharing your faith?
- Are you comfortable around unbelievers? If not, why not?
- How many unbelievers can you count who are your friends?
- How often do you spend time with them?
- Suggest some ways of sharing the gospel using Christian literature.
- Are you able to relate the Scriptures to world problems and situations in the news?

- Are you comfortable doing this in discussions with unbelievers?
- If you were to share the way to know God, what Scriptures would you use?
- How would you explain what it means to receive Christ?
- Can you explain the gospel without using "Christianese?"

CHAPTER SEVENTEEN

I'M OLDER AND WISER NOW

It Takes Faith to Grow Old Well

Great beginnings are long remembered, but there is much to be said for finishing well.

It's possible to begin our pursuit of Jesus Christ with great faith and devotion but lose our enthusiasm somewhere later in life. We may grow tired, cold, or bitter as we approach the finishing line. But Jesus has promised to be with us in all of life's seasons and to continue to perfect the work He has begun in us (Philippians1:6).

What can happen to prevent us from finishing well?

- Perhaps the way was harder than we expected and we became angry with God regarding our circumstances.
- Often we are disappointed with ourselves and others. We may have fallen into sin and been too ashamed to begin again.

- Other people may have disappointed us and we became disillusioned.
- We cannot forgive what someone has done or said.
- Because our expectations were unfulfilled, we have dropped out of the race.

"It takes more faith to grow old," a former pastor once told me. It's true that "old age is not for sissies!"

Youth Is the Best Time to Prepare for Old Age

Writing to *young people* in Ecclesiastes 12, Solomon seems to say that we should prepare to be old when we are young. Youth is the sowing time, when the seeds of our tomorrows are planted. (Don't you wish more young people knew this?)

The writer goes on to portray the aging process in poetic detail, describing the decline of various abilities, such as seeing, hearing, etc.

After writing concerning the words of the wise (verses 11 and 12), he concludes that man's "whole duty" is to fear God and keep His commandments, because God is the final judge of good and evil (verses 13 and 14).

In this sobering chapter, the writer, Solomon, reflects on the meaninglessness of life apart from God.

In 2 Timothy 4:7, the apostle Paul says that he has "finished the race" set before him by God. Our goal should be to "finish our race" in a similar manner by continuing to trust and obey the Lord.

What If I've "Blown It?"

Jenny and Sam, a middle-aged couple, came to personal faith in Christ later in life. Their youthful years of rebellion had resulted in many wrong choices. Their family life is complicated by several former husbands and wives and an assortment of children—his, hers, and theirs. Although they wish they could return to their youth and begin again, following Christ from the beginning, they cannot do that.

But Jenny and Sam know that when they came to Christ in repentance and faith, He gave them a new beginning. The past is forgiven and gone. Although there may be struggles, they can begin from where they are now to sow seeds of obedience for the future. They, like others in similar circumstances, can finish the race God has planned for them, and they can be a positive influence on their families.

Growing In Our Later Years

Psalm 92:12–15 gives four promises to the person who has claimed God's righteousness through faith in Christ. (We have no righteousness of our own.) They are as follows:

- The righteous will "flourish" (verse 12). This does not mean that we will be trouble-free, that we will never stumble, or that we will always be economically prosperous. It means that we will grow in our ability to trust and obey our Savior and find joy and fulfillment in Him, even when the way is hard.
- They will grow. In what ways can we continue to grow throughout our lifetime? Do these verses give us any hint?
- They will bear fruit in old age (verse 14). What kind of fruit do you think the writer had in mind?
- They will "stay fresh and green." What attitudes are mentioned in verse 15 that contribute to this "freshness?"

God Will be with Us

Isaiah 46:3–4 lists God's promises to Israel. Since God is unchanging in His character and loves His church (that's us), we can also claim these promises:

- We have been carried by God from before our birth—carried from the womb. If we know Christ today, it is because He predestined us from the foundation of the world (Ephesians 1:4–14).
- God will sustain us—carry us—in old age. He is the same God who has walked with us in prior years.
- He has made us, borne us, will carry us and save us. Resting in the love and sovereignty of our God should bring great assurance in every period of life, especially as we near the "finishing line."

The Death of His Saints Is Precious to God

Psalm 116:15 tells us the time of our death is precious to God. Why not? He looks forward to welcoming us home in much the same way we greet loved ones who have been away from us.

Most people today, even believers, do not like to think of pain or death. In the booklet, *An Introduction to the American Soul, Reaching Out in a Postmodern Age*, Ralph Ennis and Paula Rinehart, state

> Americans acknowledge that pain is the avenue through which God can be known, if He can be known at all. Yet we seek with dogged determination to avoid pain at all costs. Knowing God would bring us face-to-face with the pain of life, the pain of life would bring us closer to knowing God. Yet we are determined to avoid one with the other…We have fooled ourselves into thinking that

> only those who are weak and poor and needy actually need Him. Those who are rich or powerful have no need of Him, unless there is something more to be gained from Him. A major goal is to keep oneself in a condition where there is little felt need of God.[1]

The reality of death prompts us to think seriously about life and God. By avoiding thoughts and discussion of death or eternity, people try to keep God at arm's length. But death puts life in perspective.

We all have a natural fear of the unknown. We dread pain, loneliness, and the reduced functioning of our faculties in old age. Still, unless Jesus returns in our lifetime, this is the path that will lead us into His presence.

How We Can Prepare to "Finish Well?"

- Walk with God now. How do we do this?
    1. Continue to study the Bible and depend on God's promises.
    2. Work on good relationships with others.

- What other steps can we take?
    1. Accept the past and leave it with God.
    2. Plan for the future but live today.
    3. Keep your "temple" (body) in good repair. Practice good health maintenance.
    4. Embrace change. Old is not necessarily good. New is not always bad. Learn. Grow. Trust. Make every day an adventure.
    5. Accept a slower pace when circumstances require. Relax and enjoy leisure. God loves us because we're His, not because of what we do for Him.

6. Maintain a positive attitude. Don't allow yourself to become critical or bitter. Pray much about this.
7. Make friends with people of all ages. Continue to reach out and don't fear letting others help you.
8. Look ahead. Think in terms of beginnings. Eternity lies ahead! (See 1 Corinthians 15:12–28.)

Things to Think About or Discuss

- What kind of person do you want to be when you grow old?
- What do you fear most about aging?
- Is it wrong for a Christian to fear death?
- Who has been a role model for you in terms of growing old?

WHAT IS IT TO GROW OLD?

What is it to grow old?

To know my body is temporary,
to sense a stirring excitement within,
anticipating what is beyond.

The great adventure of eternity,
closer than before,
mine now in the embryo of faith.

In the womb, could I have dreamed of such a world as this one,
so beautiful—though flawed.

Preparations for my leaving are silently taking place within me;
My heart knows there is much, much more.

It has not entered into the heart of man
all that God has prepared for those who love Him.

—Carole Ledbetter
February, 1998

CHAPTER EIGHTEEN

I'M HAVING THE TIME OF MY LIFE

We are all having the time of our lives!

I like to think of time as a line surrounded by eternity—a line maybe an inch or two long on a white sheet of paper. Eternity is the white space. God is outside the line, but He works within it.

Scripture tells us to "number our days and apply our hearts to wisdom."

The Westminster Catechism declares that "the chief end of man is to glorify God and to enjoy him forever."

Author and pastor, John Piper, declares that, "God is most glorified in us when we are most satisfied in him."[1] I believe that is true. God doesn't take our happiness lightly. He wants us to find our satisfaction in Christ and in lives that glorify Him. When we do this, we will find joy as we journey through the time God gives us upon the earth.

"You are not the center of God's love for you. God is," says Piper, "One of the most loving commands in the Bible is, 'Behold your God.' But mankind's idea of love is, 'Behold yourself!' It puts us—the loved—at the center, permitting us to ignore God. If God loved like that, his love would be hate, because it would deprive us of the only satisfying gift he could give us—himself. But he does not! As objects of God's love, we remain peripheral, but perfectly satisfied, and he remains central—perfectly glorified. He loves us by enabling us to enjoy exalting him forever."[2]

Using Time Wisely

You cannot save time; you can only spend it.

Our son, Dan, once commented that the years of his childhood seemed, perceptually, to be half a lifetime. It seems that way to me too. Childhood passed slowly; the days, especially the summer ones, inched along.

When I was a child, play was not structured by adults, as it often is today. I could spend my summer days any way I wished. I didn't have to rush off to sports or clubs, or even piano lessons, in the summer. I never ran out of things to do. My imagination provided me with endless ideas.

I was content just to be. I didn't run ahead of myself mentally, anticipating the future, as I do now. (However, in my retirement years, I am again learning to play.)

If I wished for Christmas, my mother would say, "You are wishing your life away." I think of her words whenever I want time to go faster.

Fulfilling Our Dreams

I have always been a dreamer, and I believe God delights to fulfill our dreams when we give them to Him. As long as we live within God's moral will, as defined in His Word, the Bible, we are free to pursue our dreams. Perhaps you call them goals, but goals are just dreams with deadlines. I believe God fulfills His will through the desires He puts in our hearts.

In my early Christian life, I struggled with the concept of God's will, especially as it concerned making decisions. Lately I have come to understand that I have great freedom within God's sovereignty; I can make choices while trusting God's Holy Spirit to guide me.

Garry Friesen, in his book, *Decision Making and the Will of God*, summarizes these basic principles for decision making:

1. In those areas specifically addressed by the Bible, the revealed commands of God (His moral will) are to be obeyed.
2. In those areas where the Bible gives no command or principle (nonmoral decisions), the believer is free and responsible to choose his own course of action. Any decision made within the moral will of God is acceptable to God.
3. In nonmoral decisions, the objective of the Christian is to make wise decisions on the basis of spiritual expediency.
4. In all decisions, the believer should humbly submit, in advance, to the outworking of God's sovereign will as it touches each decision.[3]

Friesen calls these four principles the "way of wisdom."

Embracing Change

The gospel is about change. If you belong to Christ, you are destined to be changed—transformed over a lifetime—finally becoming like Christ when you meet Him face to face.

It's more than a walk down an aisle, more than "being saved," or even changing the world; it's about how Christ transforms us as we walk with Him daily, making the spiritual side of life the priority, living transparently and authentically. It's about being teachable.

God has changed me through the people I have met, the books I have read, and the experiences and circumstances of life through which He has brought me.

Learning to embrace change is a difficult lesson. At best we accept change only after a struggle. Embracing it is another matter.

I believe it is one of the secrets of growing.

Change can make us feel we have lost control of our lives. But control is an illusion. Proverbs 16:9 tells us: "In his heart a man plans his course, but the Lord determines his steps." God is ultimately in charge, even when we think we are in control.

Realizing that change takes place within God's sovereign will makes all of life an adventure, although we may still struggle with accepting events that appear from our viewpoint to be losses.

As we move through our lives, there will be constant change. Family situations change as our children grow up and establish families of their own. Job situations change, we—or our spouse—may retire, family members die or move away, marital circumstances change, health concerns appear on the horizon. Many of these situations will appear to be losses.

Changes produce stress. We may go for years with everything seeming the same; suddenly circumstances shift and we feel off balance.

Changes come more quickly now. Before we've had time to adjust to one change, another is upon us. Adjusting to ATM machines, the Internet, DVDs, VCRs, GPS systems, and other assorted acronyms leaves us bewildered. The speed of daily activity challenges us to live at an ever faster pace. Even children become stressed by constant activity and too many choices.

Because we are safe in God's hands and His will for our lives is good, pleasing, and perfect, according to Romans 12:2, we can embrace change.

Change and decay are all about us declares the old hymn that closes: "O Thou, who changest not, abide with me."

He will abide and He does not change!

It is said that Hannah Whitall Smith, author of *A Christian's Secret of a Happy Life*,[4] saw herself as "a happy passenger in the chariot of God."

That's the way we should all see ourselves.

Who Am I Now?

It's been quite a ride!

As I work at my computer on this beautiful late summer afternoon in September 2006, I wonder where the time has gone. Sometimes I feel I must hurry if I am going to complete all the adventures He has planned for me. Then I remember that my times are in His hands, and I relax.

I came to Christ as a teenager. God and I have walked together through many happy days and a few sad ones too. I still have much to learn and He is continually changing me. Because He is unchanging, I can adapt and grow in the seasons and experiences life brings. I can live for His glory and become who He wants me to be. I can risk, and sometimes fail, too. I can walk with Him in the freedom of His love.

If you have never opened your heart and life to Jesus Christ as your Lord and Savior, would you do it now?

Jesus said, "Come to me, all you who are weary and burdened, and I will give you rest. Take my yoke upon you and learn from me, for I am gentle and humble in heart and you will find rest for your souls. For my yoke is easy, and my burden is light" (Matthew 11:28–30).

I have found it to be so.

Scripture Passages to Consider

- 1 Peter 4:10–11
- Philippians 4:11–13
- Proverbs 3:5–6
- John 1:10–13
- Hebrews 13:5
- Ephesians 2:8–10

Things to Think About or Discuss

- Do you resist change? Why?
- What change is causing stress in your life now?
- Do you think it is true that we create our own stress? Explain.
- How can God's sovereignty help you accept change?
- How do you respond to Garry Friesen's "way of wisdom?"
- How do you feel about John Piper's comment, "You are not the center of God's love for you. God is?"
- Have you invited Christ into your life to be your Lord and Savior?
- Why not do it now?

Endnotes

Chapter 1

1. E. S. Jones, *Is the Kingdom of God Realism?* (Nashville, Tennessee: Parthenon Press, 1940), page 194.

Chapter 2

1. George Beverly Shea, *Tenderly He Watches.*
2. Cynthia and Robert Hicks, *The Feminine Journey, Understanding the Biblical Stages of a Woman's Life* (Colorado Springs, Colorado: NAVPRESS 1994), page 115.

Chapter 3

1. M. Craig Barnes, *Finding Good Sex*: http://preachingtodaysermons.com.
2. Gary Chapman, *The Five Love Languages* (Chicago, Illinois: Northfield Publishing, 1992, 1995), page 14.
3. Ibid., page 38.

4. John Gray, *Men are From Mars, Women are From Venus* (New York, New York: Harper Collins 1992), page 31.
5. Ibid., page 33.
6. Gary Chapman, *Five Signs of a Loving Family* (Chicago, Illinois: Northfield Publishing, 1997), page 46.

Chapter 5

1. Nancy Ortberg, "The Jeckyll and Hyde of Motherhood," http://www.preachingtodaysermons.com.
2. Emilie Barnes, *Emilie's Creative Home Organizer* (Eugene, Oregon: Harvest House Publishers, 1995), page 194.

Chapter 6

1. Ross Campbell, *How to Really Love Your Child* (Wheaton, Illinois: Victor Books, 1977), page 12.
2. Ibid., pages 79–81.
3. Anna B. Mow, *Your Child From Birth to Rebirth* (Grand Rapids, Michigan: Zondervan, 1972), pages 27–28.
4. Ibid., page 53
5. Ibid, page 95.
6. Gary Smalley and John Trent, *The Blessing* (New York, New York: Simon & Schuster, Inc., 1986), page 17.
7. Ibid., page 106.
8. Ibid., pages 54–55.

Chapter 7

1. *Webster's New World College Dictionary*, Fourth Edition, Copyright 1999 by McMillan USA.

2. Emilie Barnes, *Emilie's Creative Home Organizer* (Eugene, Oregon. Harvest House, 1995), page 13.
3. Louise Story, *New York Times*, September 20, 2005.

Chapter 9

1. Paul J. Waddell, *Becoming Friends*, Brazos Press (July 2002).

Chapter 10

1. C. S. Lewis, *Mere Christianity* (Great Britain, Fontana Books 1952), Preface, page 12.
2. Ibid., page 12.

Chapter 12

1. *Webster's New World College Dictionary*, Fourth Edition, Copyright 1999 by Macmillan USA.

Chapter 14

1. *Webster's New World College Dictionary*, Fourth Edition, Copyright 1999 by Macmillan USA.
2. Madeleine L 'Engle, *Walking on Water, Reflections on Faith and Art* (Wheaton, Illinois, Harold Shaw Publishers, 1980), page 145.
3. E. S. Jones, *Is the Kingdom of God Realism?* (Nashville, Tennessee, Parthenon Press, 1940), page 147.
4. Diane Fassel, *Working Ourselves to Death: The High Cost of Workaholism and the Rewards of Recovery* (Harper San Francisco, a Division of Harper Collins, New York, New York, 19~), pp 3.

Chapter 15

1. Paul Tournier, *A Listening Ear, Reflections on Christian Caring* (Minneapolis, Minnesota: Augsburg, 1987), pages 9–11.
2. Ibid., page 10.
3. Ibid., page 10–11.
4. Ibid., pages 32–33.
5. Ibid., page 12.
6. *Webster's New World College Dictionary*, Fourth Edition, Copyright 1999 by McMillan USA.

Chapter 16

1. Laura Schlessinger, *The Ten Commandments* (New York, New York: Harper Collins, 1998).
2. Carole Ledbetter, "From Barroom to Ballroom," *The Standard*, January-February 1998: page 13.

Chapter 17

1. Ralph Ennis and Paula Rinehart, *An Introduction to the American Soul, Reaching Out in a Postmodem Age* (Raleigh, NC; LEAD Consulting, 1998), page 13.

Chapter 18

1. John Piper, *Future Grace*, Multnomah Publishers, Inc. (Sisters, Oregon 1995), page 72.
2. John Piper, DG Sermons: Is There a "Lord's Day"? (www.DesiringGod.org).
3. Garry Friesen with J. Robin Maxson, *Decision Making and The Will of God*, Multnomah Publishers (Sisters, Oregon), 1980, page 151.

4. Hannah Whitall Smith, *The Christian's Secret of a Happy Life* (Copyright 1983 by Whitaker House, USA).

Contact Information

To order additional copies of this book, please visit
www.redemption-press.com.
Also available on Amazon.com and BarnesandNoble.com
Or by calling toll free 1-844-2REDEEM.

CPSIA information can be obtained
at www.ICGtesting.com
Printed in the USA
FSHW012335160121
77711FS